THE FAKE AND DECEPTIVE SCIENCE BEHIND ROE V. WADE

Settled Law
v.
Settled Science

THOMAS W. HILGERS, MD

Copyright ©2020 by Thomas W. Hilgers, MD
Saint Paul VI Institute

**Library of Congress
Cataloging-in-Publication Data**

Hilgers, Thomas W, 1943–
Thomas W. Hilgers, MD

Includes bibliographical references and index.
ISBN: 978-0-825309410

**Cover Design: Matthew A. Johnson
Design and Layout: Matthew A. Johnson**

Published in the United States by:

**Beaufort
Books**

New York, New York
in association with

Distributed by Midpoint Trade Books
a division of Independent Publishers Group

Printed in China.

Table of Contents

Introduction

On January 22, 1973, the United States Supreme Court in a 7 to 2 decision, legalized abortion throughout the United States and throughout the entire course of pregnancy. This decision, written under the name of Associate Justice Harry Blackmun, is noteworthy for its *lack of scholarship, extraordinary bias, its pre-medieval approach to pregnancy-related science* and its *intellectual dishonesty*. Clearly it was a decision written out of a pro-abortion mindset. This was a Supreme Court decision that was activist through and through; it **ignored** and **purposely rejected** a period of at least 400 years of **scientific enlightenment** on the understanding of the beginning and the development of human life that existed in the womb for each one of us. Unfortunately, it followed the lead of the *American College of Obstetricians and Gynecologists (ACOG)* which presented to the Court data and concepts that one could only consider to be *false* and/or *deceptive*. The ACOG is one of the largest pro-abortion lobbying groups in the U.S. and throughout the world. **The Court's decision was anything but fair and impartial!**

Over the last 47 years, there have been well over a conservative estimate of 60 million abortions performed in the United States; it may have reached as high as 70 to 80 million. The purpose of this book is to undertake a critical investigation of the Court's scientific positioning found in *Roe v. Wade*[1] (Texas) and its companion case, *Doe v. Bolton*[2] (Georgia). It will also look at important and vital scientific work that was ignored and/or rejected by the Court while assessing the reliability of data regarding the incidence of criminal (illegal) abortion and the maternal mortality rate related to legally-induced abortion and *"normal childbirth"* (that was presented to them by the ACOG). It also discusses the dehumanizing and deceptive intervention of the ACOG on the topics of human embryology and human fetology. Furthermore, this investigation will show that the Court acted within the context of a *historically **pre-medieval approach** to pregnancy-related science* so as to justify its ruling. Lawrence Lader, who was described as "a leader of the campaign to legalize abortion" and at the time of *Roe* was Chairman (and Co-Founder) of the National Association for the Repeal of Abortion Laws (NARAL), was Blackmun's *most cited reference.*[3] Except for short sections on continued scientific advances and what has been lost, *this book focuses on what was available to the Supreme Court in 1973.*

Roe v. Wade

In Section VI of *Roe,* Blackmun says that, "Perhaps it is not generally appreciated that the restrictive criminal abortion laws in effect in a majority of states today are of relatively recent vintage. Those laws, generally proscribing abortion or its attempt at any time during pregnancy, except when necessary to preserve the pregnant woman's life, are not of ancient or even of common law origin. Instead, they derive from statutory changes effected, for the most part, in the latter half of the 19th century."[4] The decision then rejects and ignores the democratic process by which these statutes were arrived at. It was as if that process was deemed to be inferior. In justifying this, he reviewed some of the "ancient attitudes" regarding the Hippocratic Oath. In reviewing ancient attitudes, he cited the thoughts of Aristotle, Soranus of Ephesus and Galen. That took us from 460 BC to 200 AD.[5]

In discussing the Hippocratic Oath and significantly demeaning it, he *relied heavily* on L. Edelstein's book on the Oath *written in 1943 **before** the famous post World War II Nuremburg trials.* Blackmun says that Edelstein reached the conclusion that the oath originated in a group representing only a small segment of Greek opinion that was not accepted by all ancient physicians. He points out that the medical writings down to Galen, "give evidence of the violation of almost every one of its injunctions." Ultimately, Blackmun concurred with Edelstein's suggestion that it was "a Pythagorean Manifesto and not the expression of an absolute standard of medical conduct." It seemed to Blackmun that this was a satisfactory and acceptable explanation of the Hippocratic Oath's "apparent rigidity."[6]

In doing this, Justice Blackmun brushed aside over 2,000 years of medical history to accept a working hypothesis of one deceased historian as gospel. Apparently, those thousands upon thousands who have taken this oath: "I will give no deadly medicine to anyone if asked, nor suggest any such counsel; and in like manner, I will not give a woman a pessary to produce abortion" are only the tools of the Pythagoreans.[7]

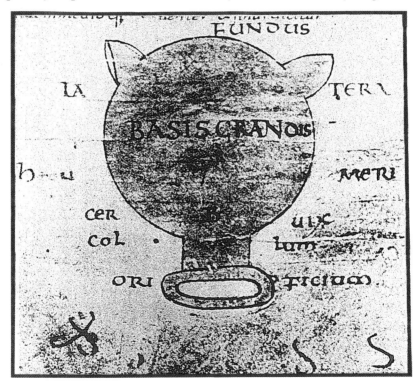

Figure Intro-1: Oldest known drawing of the uterus from a ninth-century copy of Soranus' work.[8]

Blackmun relies, in large part, on these early (ancient) physicians and philosophers to help dehumanize the early human embryo and take value away from it. He says that early philosophers believed that the embryo or fetus did not become formed and begin to live until at least 40 days after conception for a male and 80 to 90 days for a female. **But Aristotle's concepts of human procreation were truly ancient and deeply flawed.** In the Aristotelian concept, neither the ovaries nor the testicles played a role in reproduction. Aristotle taught that semen was produced in the male ducts and that the testicles were weights to keep the ducts straight.[8] Blackmun goes on to discuss the common law and in that discussion brings in St. Augustine and St. Thomas Aquinas. That goes back to 354 AD and up to 1274 AD. **But knowledge of human reproduction at that stage of history was also not accurate; and, in fact, was steeped in ignorance.** For example, in **Figure Intro-1**, the oldest known drawing of a uterus from a 9th century copy of Soranus' original work is shown. **It is anatomically inaccurate.**[8]

A review of the major discoveries in reproductive function shows multiple noteworthy items: The discovery of the sperm cell and the discovery of the human egg; the sperm cell was not discovered until 1677 by Anton van Leeuwenhoek, the inventor of the microscope. He called them "Seminal animalcules." It was his thought that in the head of the sperm, there was a "little man" or "homunculus."[9] This was the visual concept of the sperm as it was imagined in the minds of scientists at the end of the 17th century **(Figure Intro-2)**. The mammalian egg was not seen for the first time until 1827 and that was in a dog and from the ovaries of other mammals.[10] The human egg was not seen until about 1935, but long before *Roe*.

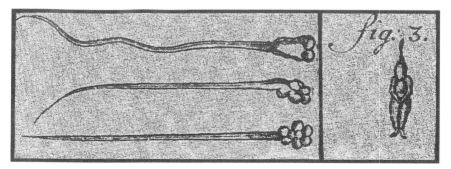

Figure Intro-2: Left, sketches of sperms as van Leeuwenhoek thought he saw them in 1677 with the aid of his newly invented microscope. Right, "homunculus" or "little man" as sperms were imagined to be in the minds of some scientists at the end of the 17th century. (Illustrations printed from woodcuts in Phil. Trans. Royal Society of London, 1677 and 1678; and as seen in Hartman CG: Science and the Safe Period. Williams and Wilkins Company, Baltimore, 1962).

While ignoring that the state of the embryological sciences that he favored was *highly inaccurate* and *steeped in ignorance*, Blackmun stood by his idea that it was just a "theory" that a human life is present from the "moment of conception[11]" and making it appear as if this was only a doctrinal statement put forth by the Catholic Church. He ultimately states that, "In view of all this, we do not agree that, by adopting 'one theory of life,' Texas may override the rights of the pregnant woman that are at stake." And yet, this is not *a theory*, it is a *fact*! Blackmun in his arrogance came forward to conclude that, *"We need not resolve the difficult question of when life begins. When those trained in the respective disciplines of medicine, philosophy and theology **are unable to arrive at any consensus the Judiciary at this point in the development of man's knowledge** is not in a position to speculate as to the answer."*[12] This is a little bit like taking the membership of the "flat earth society" and accepting their idea that the earth is flat and considering it to be of equal or greater value to the actual fact that the earth is round. It defies the scientific reality of when life begins which was **well established and consistent at the time of *Roe*.** It was not as if Blackmun did not have access to this information. In an *Amicus Brief* submitted on behalf of another group of physicians, professors and fellows of the American College of Obstetricians and Gynecologists, it was noted that, "It is our task … to show how clearly and conclusively modern science — embryology, fetology, genetics, perinatology, all of biology — establishes the humanity of the unborn child."[13] The *Amici* then proceeded to present that science.

Blackmun gives only a glancing notice to this information when he recognizes that in support of the personhood of the fetus, "They outline in detail the **well-known facts** of fetal development" (emphasis applied). He recognizes that, "If this suggestion of personhood is established, the Appellant's case, of course, collapses for the fetus' right to life is then guaranteed specifically by the Fourteenth Amendment."[14] Blackmun recognizes that these facts are "**well known**" and yet he purposely rejects them by saying **there's no consensus**. Along with this, he clearly recognized that if these "well known" facts were accepted, then their personal desire to come down in favor of the unborn would substantially argue against the court's pro-abortion position.

Let's look at a different example. It has been noted that all cells in a malignant tumor arise from a **single cell** in which the regulatory mechanism of proliferation has been disrupted. While that single cell may not be visible to the naked eye, nor is it visible through multiple levels of cellular division, it is still cancer[15]. No one would be so foolish as to say to a woman, for example, who has breast cancer cells present but in a microscopic form that those cells can be ignored. Breast cancer is cancer from the first cancer cell forward.

In writing off what Blackmun called "one theory of life"[12] (life begins at conception) he says that this would nullify the Appellant's case collapsing the fetus' right to life by guaranteeing specifically the Fourteenth Amendment. Blackmun, by one sweep of the pen, re-wrote the modern biology of the beginning and development of human life *in utero* while at the same time, strongly suggesting that this was only a religious principle and one that need not apply to all individuals who are not of that religious persuasion. That thrust us back to a time before the middle ages by discounting the embryological science that had developed in the previous 400 years because Blackmun, along with six other Justices appeared to harbor a religious bias. It was as inept, deceptive and fake then as it is now. While denigrating the Hippocratic Oath, Blackmun also *ignored significant components of modern ethical and biological research.* These will be discussed further in this book but a partial list is given at this time:

1939	• The work of *Dr. Davenport Hooker* who filmed early embryologic movement from external stimulation which was presented to the Court through an *Amicus Brief.*
1948	• The **World Medical Association** adopted the *Declaration of Geneva* (September 1948).
1949	• *The International Code of Medical Ethics* was adopted by the **United Nations.** (October, 1949).
1959	• The **General Assembly of the United Nations** unanimously adopted the *Declaration of the Rights of the Child* (November 30, 1959).
1962	• Dr. Carl Hartman, a research consultant to the ***Margaret Sanger Research Bureau*** stated that life begins at conception.

1962 • Dr. George W. Corner, Professor Emeritus of Embryology at **Johns Hopkins University** also said that *life begins at conception.*

1964 • Dr. Alan Guttmacher, the **President of Planned Parenthood**, identified *the time of conception as the beginning of an individual's human life.*

1970 • The **World Medical Association** adopted the *Declaration of Oslo.*

1970 • The **California Medical Association** in an editorial in their medical journal cited that *life begins at conception.*

1887–1972 • Multiple specialists in embryology stated that human life begins at conception. The **consensus over these 85 years before *Roe* was striking** (See Chapters 6 and 7).

In addition to that was the question of why the Court cherry-picked the history of abortion to suit their own purposes? Why did they attempt to re-write the biological reality of when life begins?

All these are important questions and they do need to be answered. It will be supported by new information that has been provided by several new books which provide close accounts of what the goals and objectives of the pro-abortion movement were about, what was driving it and why did they choose deception and made-up "facts" to present their case (to the public) while denigrating the facts of biologic realism?

All of this will be explained further in a way that I hope will be relatively short and to the point so it can be better understood by all. To help, a glossary and an index are also included.

SPECIAL NOTE:

Throughout this book, the reader will notice the liberal use of various forms of highlighting — italics, bold, and italic bold print. This is given to highlight various phrases or comments that need to be thought about as you read. I realize that some people do not like this format, but for the author, it provides an emphasis that is important for the reader so the text can be better thought about and understood.

REFERENCES

1. *Roe v. Wade*, 314F. Supp. 1217, United States Supreme Court, No. 70-18, January 22, 1973.

2. *Doe v. Bolton*, 319F. Supp. 1048, United States Supreme Court, NO. 70-40, January 22, 1973.

3. Lader L: Abortion: beacon Press, Boston, 1966. (Beacon Press books are published under the auspices of the Unitarian Universalist Association).

4. Op. Cit. *Roe v. Wade*, p. 14.

5. Op. Cit., *Roe v. Wade*, p. 18.

6. Op. Cit., *Roe v. Wade*, p. 17.

7. Horan DJ, Gorby JD, Hilgers TW: Abortion and the Supreme Court: Death Becomes a Way of Life. In: Hilgers TW and Horan DJ, Ed: Abortion and Social Justice. Sheed and Ward, New York, 1972 (published in June 1973).

8. Gruhn JG, Kazer RR: Hormonal Regulation of the Menstrual Cycle. The Evolution of Concepts. Plenum Medical Book Company. New York and London. 1989, p. 8.

9. Hartman, Carl G: Science and the Safe Period. Williams and Wilkins Co., Baltimore, MD, p. 24.

10. Op. Cit., Gruhn and Kazer, p. 27.

11. Op. Cit, *Roe v. Wade*, pp. 35 and 47.

12. Ibid.

13. Motion and Brief, Amicus Curiae of Certain Physicians, Professors and Fellows of the American College of Obstetricians and Gynecologists in support of Appellees. In the Supreme Court of the United States, October term, 1971, No. 70-18, *Roe v. Wade* and 70-40, *Doe v. Bolton*.

14. Op. Cit., *Roe v. Wade*, p. 41.

15. Dorigo D, Berek JJ: Cancer Genetics. In: Bieber EJ, Sarafilippo JS, Horowitz IR (Eds). Clinical Gynecology, Churchill Livingstone, Philadelphia, 2006.

Chapter 1

The Investigation: Major Scientific Errors (Three out of Three)

It is often said today that *Roe v. Wade*[1] is "settled law." Sometimes this is said as a simplistic response to the question asked of a politician "What is YOUR view of *Roe v. Wade*?" However, we all know that the law is hardly ever "settled" and that changes can be made.[2] Perhaps a better and more pertinent question would be, ***"Is it settled science?"*** especially because so much of *Roe* and its companion piece, *Doe v. Bolton*[3], were built upon a science that was either *fake or deceptive*.

The Court wrote the following extraordinary, out-of-touch statement: *"We need not resolve the difficult question of when life begins. When those trained in the respective disciplines of medicine, philosophy and theology are unable to arrive at any conclusion,* the Judiciary, *at this point in man's knowledge,* is not in a position to speculate as to the answer"*[4] (emphasis applied). Yet the Court said that "the State of Texas *may not, nor may any other state,* adopt a 'theory of life' which posits the beginning of life before six months."[5] **This was a major error,** held and developed deeply out of prejudice and bias and without any consideration of the lack of sensitivity that the Court held related to the value and dignity of human life and human existence! It was the most significant of the many unscientific assessments that came out of the Court and was not up-to-date or consistent with the science or the seriousness of the issues. In addition, it is especially important to have the right answer for this question of when life begins for it is *foundational* to the ultimate future of this decision, and other decisions that may flow from it.

For many years now, I have been involved in evaluating the abortion question as it relates to the law and medicine. For example, I wrote some of the medical sections of an *Amicus Brief*[6] that was submitted to the United States Supreme Court in *Roe v. Wade* on behalf of over 150 specialists in medicine, surgery and obstetrics and gynecology. We took the position of being opposed to abortion for many different reasons. Justice Harry Blackmun, however, in his final decision, legalized abortion literally on demand and throughout the entire course of pregnancy.[1,3] Blackmun did this while either ignoring or rejecting the material presented in this *Amicus Brief*. It's hard to comprehend that 60 million abortions later this is "settled law" when it was promulgated on out-of-date science (literally from *before* the Middle Ages) and other data that was clearly biased and prejudiced in favor of abortion. (See chapters 3 through 7.)

While it is completely true that there have been a number of abortion-related cases that have been presented before the United States Supreme Court since *Roe* and *Doe*, one still needs to go *back to the original decisions* to see whether any premise was presented that is truly substantive and foundational to the court's view of their science that favors abortion. This book takes a look at all three of the major scientific issues that were identified in the Court's presentations, and all three were grossly in error.

THE THREE MAJOR SCIENTIFIC ERRORS

1. The prevalence of **high maternal mortality rates** at illegal "abortion mills" was said by the Court "to strengthen rather

than weaken the state's interest in regulating the conditions under which abortions are performed.[3]" **A frequent estimate provided to the Court by the ACOG through their *Amicus Curiae* brief was "that over one million criminal abortions occur in the United States each year, resulting in an estimated 5,000 maternal deaths annually"**[6] (and at times 5,000-10,000 maternal deaths).

2. The claim was made that the maternal mortality rate from legal abortion was **23.3 times safer** than the mortality **from normal (ordinary) childbirth.**[1]

3. The claim was also made that there was **"new embryologic data"** that **the beginning of life** is not an "event" but a "process"[7] (a **continuum literally occurring over millions of years.**[8])

With belief in all of these three claims, the United States Supreme Court made the judgement in *Roe v. Wade*[1] and its companion piece *Doe v. Bolton*[3] (January 22, 1973) that there were no compelling state interests in keeping abortion from being legalized. If these three claims were erroneous, then over 60 million new humans have been wantonly destroyed and the hearts of their mothers and the nation as a whole have been turned cold without substantial reason.

If the reader cannot imagine that such an esteemed group as the United States Supreme Court would do something like this, let me give you one simple example. In the early paragraphs of *Roe*, the Court identified "the normal **266-day human gestation period.**"[9] But the *gestation period* is calculated by definition from the first day of a woman's last menstrual period and is **280 days in length not 266.** From the time of conception measures the **"fetal age"** and is **2 weeks different than (shorter than) the gestational age.** The gestational age actually **adds** 2 additional weeks when the woman is **not** pregnant.[10] Such a basic error, while not of enormous significance in the grand scheme of things, does reveal the lack of scientific expertise on display in these decisions.

While *Roe v. Wade* (and by association *Doe v. Bolton*) has led to the claim that this now is "settled law," the question that is asked in this book is whether or not it is **settled science** and if it is not, then how could it actually be settled law? How did the Court go about doing its research on this subject? Was it consistent with the scientific knowledge in existence in 1973 and was it consistent with the principles of scientific inquiry? If submitted to a medical journal, would it meet the rigorous demands of peer review (absent political spin)? Has anything changed since 1973 that could bolster or reinforce the Court's position or has science established the Court's assessment with greater strength. Was the Court's exploration of the science a serious effort consistent with the seriousness of this issue or was it a presentation that literally left out the science on the growth and development of every human being that existed in the world in 1973 or now in 2020?

This book will go into detail regarding these three major scientific errors that were prominent and considered infallible in *Roe* and *Doe*. Furthermore, it will be shown that those who professionally supported these three errors did so through the **distortion of scientific reality** and the **denial of biologic realism** while presenting it **deceptively** to the Court and to the nation.

There were three main people who appear to have been major sources in the writing and research of *Roe v. Wade* that were themselves obsessed with abortion and leaders in an activist movement to promote abortion and its legalization. These three were Dr. Bernard Nathanson, Lawrence Lader and Cyril Means, Jr. I will go into some detail about these three individuals, their background, their motivations and their personal positions on the abortion issue (as opposed to being neutral and/or objective). Who actually wrote *Roe* and *Doe?* Supposedly it was Justice Harry Blackmun, but was it? As each section is concluded, the question will be asked as to whether or not the analysis is "fake," "deceptive" or "accurate." **This is a serious effort and it should be taken seriously!**

CHAPTER 1
REFERENCES AND FOOTNOTES

1. *Roe v. Wade*, 314 F Supp. 1217, U.S. Supreme Court No. 70-18, January 22, 1973.

2. Wolf, R: Nothing Sacred About Legal Precedent. USA Today, Oct. 4, 2018, p. 4A.

3. *Doe v. Bolton*, 319 F Supp. 1048, U.S. Supreme Court No. 70-40, January 22, 1973.

4. Op. Cit., *Roe v. Wade*, p. 44.

5. Op. Cit., *Roe v. Wade*, p. 47.

6. *Roe, Doe and Doe v. Wade*, 70-18, October Term, 1970, Brief *Amicus Curiae* of Certain Physicians, Professors and Fellows of the American College of Obstetrics & Gynecology, The American Psychiatric Association, The American Medical Association, The New York Academy of Medicine, and a group of 178 physicians as *Amicus Curiae* in support of Appellants.

7. Op. Cit., *Roe v. Wade*, p. 45.

8. Op. Cit., *Roe v. Wade*, p. 46 (FN, 62).

9. Op. Cit., *Roe v. Wade*, p. 10

10. Hellman, LM and Pritchard, JA: Williams Obstetrics 14th Edition, Appleton-Century- Cross Educational Division/Meredith Corporation, New York, NY, 1971, p. 199.

> "The different terms commonly used to indicate the duration of pregnancy and fetal age are somewhat confusing. *Menstrual age* or *gestational age* commences on the first day of the last menstrual period before conception, or about two weeks before ovulation and fertilization, or nearly three weeks before implantation fo the fertilized ovum. As pointed out in Chapter 8 (246), about 280 days, or 40 weeks elapse on the average between the first day of the last menstrual period and delivery of the infant. Two hundred eighty days correspond to 9-1/3 calendar months or

10 units of 28 days each. The unit of 28 days has been commonly but imprecisely referred to as a lunar month of pregnancy, since the time from one new moon to the next is actually 29-1/2 days. It is the usual practice for the obstetrician to calculate the duration of pregnancy on the basis of menstrual age. Embryologists, however, cite events in days or weeks from the time of ovulation (*ovulation age*) or conception (*conception age*), the two being nearly identical. Occasionally it is of some value to divide the period of gestation into 3 units of 3 calendar months each, or 3 *trimesters*, since some important obstetric events may be conveniently categorized by trimesters. For example, the possibility of spontaneous abortion is limited almost entirely to the first trimester of pregnancy, whereas the likelihood of survival of the prematurely born infant is generally confined to pregnancy that reached the third trimester."

Chapter 2

Why Cherry-Pick the History?

When appraising or evaluating any question of science, having a historical perspective is actually very important and helpful because things can change from one moment to the next or one century to the next and that may give a person or a group of people definite insight into the perspective of the science that they are looking at. For example, Ignaz Semelweiss was the physician who discovered that the maternal mortality rate was much higher in childbirth when those women were delivered by physicians than it was when they were delivered by midwives.[1] You might think that this is somewhat strange because in general physicians are supposed to know what they're doing. But on many occasions, in those days, the doctor would walk out of the autopsy room with hands still dirty from the autopsy and then walk into the delivery room to deliver a baby. Dr. Semelweiss identified the fact that the midwives were not doing autopsies and were washing their hands before they delivered a baby. So, he speculated that there must be something being brought from the autopsy room to the delivery room which might contaminate the delivery and make it more perilous for the women.

Of course, he was correct! But Semelweiss was very strong in his sense of understanding what was fundamentally happening in these situations and he expressed it in a way which was also relatively strong trying to get people to change their point of view. The medical profession, as one can imagine, would not be very receptive to that type of an approach, but Semelweiss felt very strongly about this — as he should have — but the physicians began to label him as mentally unfit and the women continued to die. It wasn't until bacteria were identified and seen as a cause of some of these difficulties and problems that a paradigm shift occurred. At that time, the doctors changed their approach, and there was a decrease to some extent at least, in their maternal mortality rates.

So looking at history is not a bad thing and something that I personally admire. However, you can't look at history while wearing glasses that are foggy, maybe even very foggy. For that matter, the view might also be biased or prejudiced in some way. Ultimately, that's what the Supreme Court did in *Roe v. Wade*[2] and *Doe v. Bolton*.[3] They looked at the history with glasses that were designed to see only those things that would defend their preexisting point of view that abortion should be legalized. Of course, I'm speaking figuratively here and not literally. There really were no "glasses" as such but there were strongly-biased and prejudicial thought processes that distorted their selective evaluation of history.

In *Roe v. Wade,* for example, there was one section that was related to the historical aspects of this issue and it was by far the longest section (18 pages).[4] One of these had to do with a look at the perspectives of ancient physicians, philosophers and theologians; for example, Hippocrates, Aristotle, Soranus of Ephesus (who incidentally was identified as the world's greatest gynecologist by Blackmun), Galen, St. Augustine and St. Thomas Aquinas **(Table 2-1)**. This spanned a period of time from about 460 B.C. to 1274 A.D. a period of more than 1,700 years. Blackmun was trying to get a sense of what their perspective on the developing unborn child and abortion might be. After these nearly 18 centuries, there was published an illustration of a child in the womb which was *stylized* and reflected the medieval resistance to biologic realism that existed at the time **(Figure 2-1)**. The Supreme Court in their historical approach basically kept this notion of medieval resistance instead of rejecting it. *They kept us all historically in an age in 1973 that was **pre-medieval**, adopting it as the Supreme Court's view of this history.*

TABLE 2-1

U.S. SUPREME COURT'S DECISION ON THE DENIAL OF PERSONHOOD TO THE UNBORN *(ROE v. WADE)* BASED UPON THE FOLLOWING PHYSICIANS, PHILOSOPHERS AND THEOLOGIANS[1]

Name[1]	Time Period of Their Life
Hippocrates	460–370 B.C.
Aristotle	384–322 B.C.
Soranus of Ephesus	98–138 A.D.
Galen	129–200 A.D.
St. Augustine	354–430 A.D.
St. Thomas Aquinas	1225–1274 A.D.

1. From: *Roe v. Wade,* 314 F. Supp. 1217, United States Supreme Court, No. 70-18, January 22, 1973

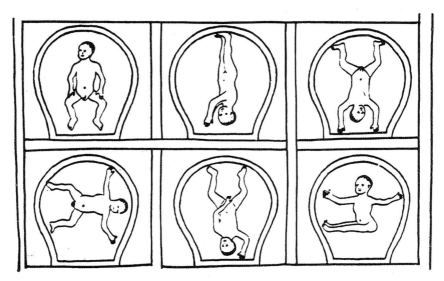

Figure 2-1: A 15th-century illustration of a child in the womb was typically stylized and reflects the medieval resistance to biological realism (From: Flanagan, GL: The First Nine Months of Life, Simon and Schuster, New York, 1962, p. 11).

The second part of their history had to do almost completely with the evaluation of the law and its approach to abortion and the unborn child. *Keep in mind that if one doesn't make the switch to biologic realism which occurred at the beginning of the 16th century and follow the science as it developed at that point, the interpretations of the ancient philosophers, theologians and physicians become virtually irrelevant and worthless in formulating an opinion.* An example might be that while Thomas Aquinas was very much against abortion,[5] he was painted as an individual who thought that the soul came into the male baby at 40 days and into the female baby at 80 days. It would certainly be observed in our current view that this would be strikingly prejudicial against females. Furthermore, while a significant amount of energy has gone into disputation regarding the existence of the soul, or when the soul is infused into the human body, this all amounts to pure conjecture and faith since the soul has never been seen.

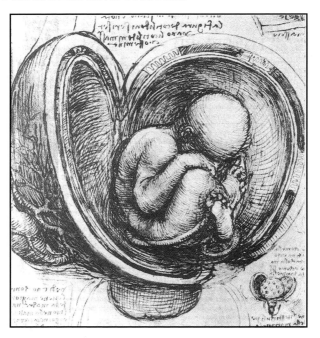

Figure 2-2: Leonardo da Vinci sketched the unborn infant in his notebooks of 1510–1512. "Do you see how the great vessels of the mother pass into the uterus," he wrote in his customary left-handed mirror writing. The bottom line … indicates that he wrongly believed this infant had no need of a beating heart because it was "vivified and nourished by the life of the mother." [Royal Collection, Windsor Castle, copyright reserved] (From: Flanagan GL, The First Nine Months of Life, Simon and Schuster, New York, 1962, p. 8).

Having believed all of that, *Roe v. Wade* then moves into the history of the courts from Common Law in England to legal approaches in the United States while denying the advances that were made in understanding the unborn infant from the first sketch of Leonardo Da Vinci in 1510 to 1512 **(Figure 2-2)** to the more recent evaluations of Davenport Hooker (See Chapter 7). Hooker[5] was able to film the response of early human embryos to outside stimulation at as early as six weeks conceptional age. He also observed *spontaneous movement* of the early embryo. This was first published in 1939.[6] There were many other events from the late 19th century up to and including the years just preceding *Roe v. Wade* that had to do with the beginning of life and its early development.

In addition to that, there were many scientific discoveries in reproductive function over the 420 years from the time of Da Vinci's sketch of the unborn infant up until the time of Davenport Hooker. Much of this was placed into a book which was published in 1962 by Geraldine Lux Flanagan and is one of the very best books available on the beginnings of life and was well within the reach — all by itself — of the United States Supreme Court. But again, it was not looked at, not recognized and completely ignored.

In Table 2-2, there are a number of major scientific discoveries in reproductive anatomy and function that are noted and the year in which they were first described from the year 1510 through 1939. This went even further with the work of Professor E. Blechschmidt, the famous German embryologist who put together a model of human growth and development which has led to the acceptance of this model by scientists.[7]

In the historic look at scientific discoveries, perhaps one of the most impressive was the book put together by Dr. William Hunter on "*The Anatomy of the Human Gravid Uterus.*"[8] Dr. Hunter was the chief physician to the Queen of England and in 1774 he published a book which showed some of the most beautiful drawings of the growth and development of the baby *in utero* from the very earliest days of development through the time of birth. The drawings are exquisite (keep in mind they didn't have photography at this time). But this did have a major impact on how scientists began to look at human growth and development *in utero* (see Chapter 7). **It was completely ignored by the Court**. The mammalian egg was first observed in 1827 although the human egg was somewhat later than that (circa 1935) and Gustov Born identified that the corpus luteum in the ovary was a gland of internal secretion particularly impressive in its production of progesterone which is the hormone that maintains pregnancy (1901).

TABLE 2-2

TIMELINE FOR MAJOR SCIENTIFIC DISCOVERIES IN REPRODUCTIVE ANATOMY AND FUNCTION[1]

Name	Discovery	Year
Leonardo Da Vinci[2]	Sketched the human unborn	1510–1512
Gabriele Falloppio	1st described oviducts	1561
Steno of Copenhagen	Substituted "ovary" for "female testicle"	1667
Reinier de Graaf	1st described ovarian follicles (rabbit)	1672
Antonie van Leeuwenhoek	1st described "seminal animalcules"	1677
William Hunter[3]	The Anatomy of the Human Gravid Uterus	1774
Karl Ernst von Baer	Discovered mammalian egg (mammals)	1827
Gustav Born	The corpus luteum was a gland of internal secretion (progesterone)	1901
Professor Ernest Starling	First introduced the term "hormone"	1905
Unknown	Human egg first seen	Circa 1935
Davenport Hooker[4]	Response of early human embryos to outside stimulation	1939–1952

1. From: Hilgers W: Anatomy and Physiology: A Primer for the **Fertility**Care™ Practitioner. Pope Paul VI Institute Press, Omaha, NE, 2002.
2. In Flanagan GL: The First Nine Months of Life. At Touchstone Book, Simon and Schuster, New York, Second Edition, 1962, p. 8.
3. Hunter W: The Anatomy of the Human Gravid Uterus: Exhibited in Figures. Birmingham by John Baskerville, London, 1774.
4. Hooker, Davenport: A Preliminary Atlas of Early Human Fetal Activity. University of Pittsburgh School of Medicine, the Ladd Laboratory of the Department of Anatomy, 1939.

This amounts to a discussion by the Court of the science of human growth and development *in utero* which **virtually ignores and is condescending in its attitude towards those who know otherwise** *(an intellectual arrogance).* Thus, it was important that Blackmun keep his science evaluation to before the middle ages rather than bringing it forward. Furthermore, the emphasis on the law during this time was simply an example of how the law persisted in keeping the science out of it (over many centuries).

Blackmun did call it conception — the beginning of human life — but classified it as "one theory of life." He also noted that Catholics **"believe"** that life begins at conception which is a misstatement of Catholic teaching. Catholics **know** that life begins at conception. It is not a belief although I would grant that knowledge can be a source for some belief. But for Catholics, for example, to see that Christ is present in the Eucharist is a belief and it does not lend itself very well to scientific evaluation. That's why they call it faith. But that's not what we're talking about here. We're talking about the beginning of human life and *the Court took an approach which ultimately is indefensible and has absolutely no foundation in science* which is the only objective source.

So to look at the history of our understanding of *in utero* human growth and development, the Court presented *very deceptive findings* which were also *ultimately fake.* They did this by ignoring the major accomplishments of science over a 400+-year period of time. I refer to this as an **"Age of Enlightenment"** when it comes to these developments.. The American people cannot make good judgments about this without the real scientific facts of this knowledge. This will be discussed in much greater detail in Chapters 5, 6, and 7.

What is really pertinent here is that when "those trained in the respective disciplines of *medicine, philosophy and theology* are unable to arrive at any consensus, the Judiciary *at this point in man's knowledge*, is not in a position to speculate as to the answer,"[10] (emphasis applied) Blackmun purposely left out the most important information and knowledge that is critical to our understanding: By leaving out the historical perspective as it existed **"at this point in man's knowledge" (January 22, 1973)**, his review of philosophy and theology ending at **1274 A.D.** and his review of the "medicine" (i.e. science) ending at **200 A.D.** when the knowledge and understanding of prenatal life and existence was virtually unknown to any extent. What became known during the 400 years before *Roe* and especially the 200 years before *Roe* (and has grown even more since 1973) appears to have been completely and purposely ignored! This left the historical review in *Roe* designed to *deceive* and to be used as a promotion of their own point of view. **Blackmun's historical review of the science was pre-medieval** and there is really no way he was not aware of this. This perspective was designed to justify the Court's final pro-abortion decision while lending its entire weight and stature to a premise which ultimately was not consistent with the science in 1973. This was an abuse of the power given to the Court at this level and does not reflect the seriousness of this decision and the impact that it would have.

CHAPTER 2
REFERENCES AND FOOTNOTES

1. Semmelweis, Ignaz Philip (1818-1865), a Hungarian physician who in Vienna (1847-1849) proved that puerperal fever is a form of septicemia, thus becoming the pioneer of anti-sepsis in obstetrics. Semmelweis' methods were not fully recognized until about 1890 even though the contagiousness of puerperal fever had been affirmed earlier. From: Dorland's Illustrated Medical Dictionary, W. B. Saunders Co., Philadelphia. 1965 and 1974, p 1505 (27th Edition).

2. *Roe v. Wade*, 314 F Supp. 1217, United States Supreme Court, No. 70-18, January 22, 1973.

3. *Doe v. Bolton*, 319 F Supp. 1048, United States Supreme Court, No. 70-40, January 22, 1973.

4. Op. Cit. *Roe v. Wade*, January 22, 1973, p. 14-32.

5. Quick Questions on St. Thomas Aquinas: http://www.catholic. com/quickquestions … "Since abortion violates natural law whether or not the child has a soul, Aquinas taught that abortion is always gravely wrong."

6. Hooker, Davenport: A Preliminary Atlas of Early Human Fetal Activity. University of Pittsburgh School of Medicine, the Ladd Laboratory of the Department of Anatomy, 1939.

7. Blechschmidt, E: Human Being from the Very First (translated by Ernst J. Brehm). In: Hilgers TW, Horan DJ and Mall D: New Perspectives on Human Abortion. Aletheia Books, University Publications of American, Frederick, MD, 1981. (Work done 1930-1972.)

8. Hunter W: The Anatomy of the Human Gravid Uterus: Exhibited in Figures. Birmingham by John Baskerville, London, 1774. Reprinted in The Classics of Obstetrics and Gynecology Library, Special Edition, 1991.

9. *Roe v. Wade*, January 22, 1973, p. 47.

10. *Roe v. Wade*, January 22, 1973, p. 44.

Chapter 3

The Problem with the U.S. Supreme Court's View of Illegal (Back-Alley) Abortion

It has always been a great joy for me to take care of women who are pregnant and to deliver their babies. I've always felt that I was the member of a profession that was especially graced by the opportunity to provide safe healthcare for women who are pregnant. I had a cousin's mother who died in childbirth and that really wasn't all that long ago. I have told a number of people over the years that things can happen more quickly in the delivery room than perhaps any place in medicine (and that would include the emergency room and the operating room). In Figure 3-1, one can see the reduction in the ratio (per 100,000 live births) of women who died in childbirth from the year 1775 all the way up through 2013. A great deal of progress has been made in this field over these last 200+ years with rapid improvement in the last century. I have personally been blessed by not ever having a woman die as a result of her pregnancy. But there have been, indeed, very complex situations which were successfully treated due to advanced medical training. Having said that, while the profession has made great strides in this particular area, the very concept of maternal death has now been used against pregnant women and their babies.

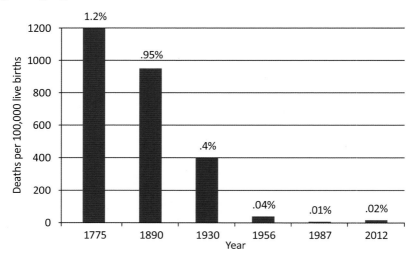

Figure 3-1: Maternal Mortality in Deaths per 100,000 live Births. Data from the US only. Previous data may or may not be from the United States only (see below).

For data from 1987 to 2012: Center for Disease Control and Prevention. Pregnancy Mortality Surveillance System. U.S. Department of Health and Human Services. January 21, 2018. http://www.cdc.gov/reproductivehealth/maternalinfanthealth/p,ss.html

For data from 1775-1956: Gibbs RS: Impact of Infectious Diseases on Women's Health: 1776-2026, Obstet Gynecol 97:1019-1023, 2001. Gibbs RS does not specify whether data is from the US only. Their sources for this data are: Shorter E. A History of Women's Bodies. New York. Basic Books, 1982.

Bureau of the Census with the Cooperation of the Social Service Research Council. Historical statistics of the United States, colonial times to 1957. Washington DC: United States Government Printing Office, 1960.

Leavitt JW: Brought to bed. Childbearing in America, 1750-1950. New York: Oxford University Press, 1986.

In the lead up to *Roe v. Wade* it was argued that there were *5,000 to 10,000 maternal deaths per year due to illegal abortion* and yet as one goes through the data on these years, there is **absolutely no evidence** of that, only the admission that **it was fabricated**. In **Table 3-1**, the number of maternal deaths due to all types of abortion (spontaneous and induced, legal or not) from 1960 through 1978 in the United States

TABLE 3-1

ESTIMATED NUMBER OF MATERNAL DEATHS DUE TO ABORTION (ALL CAUSES)[1,2]

1960–1977

Year	Estimated Number of Maternal Deaths[1,2] (Abortion all causes)	Year	Estimated Number of Maternal Deaths[1,2] (Abortion all causes)
1960	241	1969	115
1961	271	*1970	109
1962	253	1971	75
1963	234	1972	48
1964	207	*1973	25
1965	197	1974	14
1966	159	1975	14
1967	135	1976	10
*1968	99	1977	10

* = The three major dates where legalized abortion was introduced.

1. From: Hilgers TW and O'Hare, D: "Abortion Related Maternal Mortality: An In-Depth Analysis." In: Hilgers TW, Horan DJ and Mall B: New Perspectives on Human Abortion. University Publications of America, Frederick, MD, 1981, Ch. 7.

2. National Center for Vital Statistics, 1960–1977.

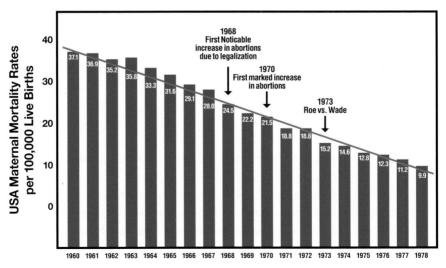

Figure 3-2: Maternal Mortality Rates — USA 1960–1978 (From: Maternal Mortality Statistics, National Center for Health Statistics, 1960–1978)

are shown. The beginning of legalized abortion (1968), the first marked increase in legal abortion in the United States (1970) and the impact of *Roe v. Wade* (1973) are all noted and yet there's been no dramatic decline in the number of maternal deaths because of the implementation of legal abortion. If there were, in fact, thousands upon thousands of women who died from illegal abortion, an abrupt decrease would show up in this data after legalization. The actual maternal mortality rates are shown in **Figure 3-2**. Instead, the decrease continued at the *well-established rate* that existed *before* abortion was legalized. **Legalization had no impact!**

In 1958, a Planned Parenthood conference on abortion in the United States concluded that "a plausible estimate of the frequency of illegal abortion in the United States could be as low as 200,000 and as high as 1.2 million ... there is no objective basis for the selection of a particular figure between these two estimates. ..."[1]

At the *First International Conference on Abortion,* held in Washington, D.C., *in 1967,* the conclusion was reached that the figures on the number of criminal abortions in the United States are "based on personal estimates" and that "no way has yet been found of obtaining reliable statistics that would give an exact figure for the total population."[2]

In Lawrence Lader's book, *Abortion,* this was at the front of his argument for abortion on pages 2 and 3: "In 1957, a conference of expats sponsored by the Planned Parenthood Federation estimated that U.S. abortions could run from 200,000 to 1,200,000 annually. Dr. Christopher Tietze, of the National Committee on Maternal Health who headed this statistical panel, considers 1,200,000 the most accurate figure today" (But Tietze never made illegal abortion an object of his own study). Lader, in the same paragraph, increased the estimate to 1,500,000 per year.[3,4]

Lader went on: "When a great number of women each year are forced into the hands of private abortionists, the result is a shocking toll in injuries and fatalities ..." It was estimated that "5,000 to 10,000 abortion deaths" occurred annually.[3] It was noted that New York City was *"the only major municipality keeping full abortion statistics and applied proportionate to population to the rest of the country"*[5] (emphasis applied). **This is actually a very important statement because it is *not likely* that data on this topic from New York City is transferrable to**

the United States as a whole, and this was, in fact, what was being done.

It has been difficult to get to the true statistics. Dr. Mary S. Calderone wrote in 1960 that: "The best statistical experts we could find would only go so far as to estimate that, on the basis of present studies, the frequency of illegally-induced abortion in the United States might be as low as 200,000 and as high as 1,200,000 per year. During the course of the conference, however, it was notable that the figure of 1,000,000 abortions yearly, or one for every four births in the United States, was advanced again and again by the various participants. ... therefore ... whether the incidence is as low as 200,000 or as high as 1,200,000, nevertheless, we do have an illegal abortion problem."

Should public health people look upon it as a problem? Can they shrug off even 200,000 invasions of pregnant uteri as of no medico-social importance? [1] But one can say that less than 100 maternal deaths from *all types* of abortions were reported in the two years before *Roe*.

Later, Dr. Kenneth R. Niswander, in a paper published in the Case Western Reserve Law Review in 1965 said that: "... criminal abortion currently accounts for *thousands of deaths annually* in the United States"[6] (emphasis applied). But no citation was given for this number. The number of deaths in his estimate grew from 1960 until 1965 without any additional research or verification.

Dr. Bernard Nathanson, the former Medical Director of the largest abortion clinic in the U.S. and a Co-Founder of the National Association for the Repeal of Abortion Laws (NARAL), wrote in 1979 in his book, *Aborting America:* "How many deaths were we talking about when abortion was illegal? In NARAL, we generally emphasized the frame of the individual case, not the mass statistics, but when we spoke of the latter, it was always 5,000 to 10,000 deaths per year. *I confess that I knew that the figures were totally false* (emphasis applied) and I suppose that others did too if they stopped to think of it. But in the morality of our revolution, it was a useful figure, widely accepted, so why go out of our way to correct it with honest statistics? The overriding concern was to get the laws eliminated, and anything within reason that had to be done was permissible."[7] But in September, 2018, in a pro-abortion talk, Chelsea Clinton went on to emphasize the tragedy of illegal abortion if we were ever to make abortion illegal again.[8] One of the major factors in presentations such as this is the complete absence of a discussion of the potential impact that programs with positive alternatives could likely produce. If we can make a major decrease in smoking with such programs, it is very likely that these types of programs could reduce the number of illegal abortions if ever implemented.

Figure 3-3

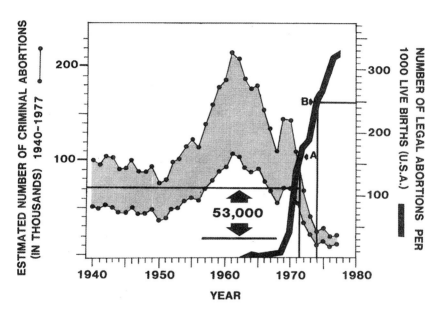

Figure 3-3: The estimated number of criminal abortions in the United States for the years 1940-1977 = stippled area.[9] The number of legal abortions per 1,000 live births (legal abortion ratio) for the United States 1963-1977 = bold bar. The horizontal line represents comparable time periods (based on birth rates). A decline in criminal abortions was not observed until the legal abortion ratio reached approximately 160 (point A) and no further decline has been observed for the legal abortion ratio above approximately 250 (point B). The graph demonstrates the average reduction in criminal abortions of 53,000 observed as the result of legalized abortion, and an estimated 50,000 to 220,000 illegal abortions with an annual average of 98,000. This is far less than previous nonobjective models.[9]

The estimated average number of illegal abortions per year over this 33-year period was 98,000 (Figure 3-3). In addition, an estimated annual decrease in the number of illegal abortions brought about through legalization of abortion was a modest four-fold decrease. However, this required an **18.4 times increase** in the number of legal abortions to accomplish this.

The National Center for Vital Statistics (NCVS) keeps excellent records on maternal deaths and it is very unlikely for them to miss them. Certainly, it can happen, but it would be a very small percentage. The author and colleagues did an in-depth study of this using an objective model for estimating the number of illegal abortions annually in the U.S.[9] This is the data shown in Figure 3-3.

Furthermore, Table 3-1 shows the best estimate for **the number of maternal deaths from all causes of abortion.** In 1973, the actual year of *Roe v. Wade*, there were 25 maternal deaths. In 1972, 48 and 75 in 1971. In 1965, it was 197 and in 1960, 241.[9] This is **far less** than what was given to the American public in the years before *Roe v. Wade* and to the U.S. Supreme Court to help them decide *Roe v. Wade* and *Doe v. Bolton*. This shows an ongoing decrease due basically to improved medical care. As indicated above, ***the data given to the public and the Court was falsified on purpose. And, the Supreme Court fell for it!***

A PERSONAL ACCOUNT

I have always wondered deeply about what motivates a woman to go to an illegal abortionist when she knows clearly what the medical risks are. I have often said publicly that these women are *socially aborted* in advance of their medical abortion and that, more than anything else drives them to the abortionist.[10] But, having said that, in all of my years of training in obstetrics and gynecology and also the practice of it, I have actually only seen one patient who attempted an illegal abortion. My training at the University of Minnesota Medical School and later in my residency in obstetrics and gynecology at the Mayo Graduate School of Medicine, did not offer much experience in the way of medical situations such as this. However, as part of my Mayo training, I took six months in obstetrics at Cook County Hospital in Chicago. It was there that I encountered the first and only person that I know of that attempted an illegal abortion and subsequent consequences from it. Let me share this incredible story with you.

It was about 8 to 9:00 p.m. one night when I was on call and the emergency room paged me to come see a woman who appeared to be quite sick; she was 18 weeks pregnant and had a fever of 103.6° F. I went down to see her, introduced myself and talked to her about the situation that she was in. In her case, she had been to an illegal abortionist who had surgically manipulated the cervix and then gave her some medicine that was supposed to treat her "pregnancy." She developed some problems following this within a few days and went back to the abortionist who gave her a prescription for an antibiotic which virtually did not help her situation at all.

When I saw her in the emergency room, she did have a high fever, her abdomen was very, very tender, she had rebound tenderness and the uterus was about 18 weeks in size. These signs and symptoms — along with the fever — are characteristic of *acute chorioamnionitis* — an infection that is present in the membranes and within the uterus surrounding the pregnancy. I was interested in knowing whether or not the baby had survived this so I retrieved a 1972 version of a Doppler unit that I could listen to the baby's heartbeat (if it was present). I put it on her abdomen and, indeed, the heartbeat was present at 180 beats per minute. I honestly did not know what to do at that moment. We had been taught — and I might add young doctors are today still being taught this — that the only treatment is to empty the uterus. So I knew that the approach would be to start by giving her Pitocin, putting her in labor and in effect emptying the uterus.

But I wondered to myself, why would we do that when maybe we could treat the mother directly for this infection with antibiotics. So I gave her very high doses of ampicillin and gentamicin being the only antibiotics that would give us a sufficient amount of coverage (most of the time at least) in a case like this. Of course, I admitted her to the hospital as well.

The next morning, the abdomen was still tender, there was still some rebound, but there was an area the size of a silver dollar on top of her abdomen which was no longer tender and her temperature had normalized. This gave me some hope that we might be successful with this treatment. So I continued the treatment and each day when I rounded on her (usually twice a day), the uterus became less and less tender and by the 9th or 10th day of her hospitalization, the uterus was completely non-tender. There were no signs of infection present anymore.

During this period of time in the hospital, I got to know this woman and had a number of good conversations with her about all of this; and I could see that her heart was beginning to warm to this baby. When I discharged her, or shortly thereafter at least she told me that she would be moving to Detroit and the baby would be born there. I was a little disappointed I must admit because I had hoped I could deliver this baby, but I kept in touch with her even though she moved to Detroit and she eventually had a baby girl who was very healthy and was delivered at full term. Here is the incredible comment that she made to me at that time. I asked her what she was going to name the baby and while I do not remember the exact name because it was a name I was not familiar with, she indicated to me that the name meant "looking forward to the baby coming."

So here I had a woman who had undergone an attempted illegal abortion where nobody intervened in her life in a positive way, she became very ill because of the instrumentation of the uterus, she was significantly infected and I broke protocol to see if we could treat her. To my amazement, the treatment was successful at getting rid of the chorioamnionitis and, at the same time, seeing that it was successfully treated and also she responded to somebody who, in the natural course of events, had befriended her. It was a remarkable moment not only in my life, but in that woman's life and in this baby's life. It didn't take a lot to accomplish this except breaking away from the culture of obstetrics that says these pregnancies cannot be treated successfully and the teaching of emptying the uterus which is still prevalent in today's world with this type of a condition. In fact, **this approach to treatment is literally a 19th Century approach** that has changed very little in the last century. But also, it taught me that if you can simply care a little bit about the plight of a woman like this, and introduce more effective treatments aimed at the root medical issues, you might actually be able to make a difference in her life and in the life of her baby.

So a lot of what you hear about illegal and criminal abortion, while it is serious from a medical point of view, is something that can be impacted medically to a true and good outcome. In fact, I have turned that experience into an effective treatment for the reduction and/or elimination of preterm labor in patients who have a silent chorioamnionitis. This has been discussed in detail in my textbook, *The Medical & Surgical Practice of* **NaProTECHNOLOGY**[11]; but still it is being avoided and these patients go without adequate treatment. There is absolutely no question in my mind that adequate treatment can be given to most of these patients which will not harm them and can also save their life along with saving their baby's. This story suggests that as a profession, we can do so much better of relating to these people who have had these experiences instead of being paralyzed by a woman who is in this plight.

So is the approach to illegal or back-alley abortion, sometimes referred to as "coat-hanger" abortion, really factual or has it been fabricated? The total number of illegal abortions in the United States was far less than what was cited by the Court. We did a study a number of years ago that showed that using an objective model, the number of illegal abortions per year ran between about 50,000 and 200,000, with the average being closer to the 98,000 per year.[9] Furthermore, once abortion was legalized, it did not eliminate all illegal abortions but there was a reduction of about 53,000; having said that, it also means that about 18 legal abortions would be necessary to eliminate one illegal abortion, and that, from a medical point of view, is a highly inefficient approach and, of course a violent and destructive one to solve these issues. Ultimately, it comes back to a major question and that is, does abortion really solve any problem, whether legal or illegal and, while on the surface, many might say, "Yes!" to that question, the everyday experience suggests that social and economic problems, psychological problems and others **cannot be helped with a surgical procedure aimed at emptying the uterus.** In fact, the healing that can go on with a pregnancy such as that can be quite positive if she keeps the baby or carries the baby to full term and adopts it out. The *social abortion* that I mentioned earlier needs to be eliminated (see Figure 5-1, Chapter 5).

The data on maternal deaths due to illegal abortion was fabricated — it is fake! And it has always been fake. The deaths from abortion in the United States were (all types: spontaneous and induced, legal or illegal) 25 in the year 1973, 48 in 1972 and 75 in 1971, not 5,000 or 10,000.

CHAPTER 3
REFERENCES

1. Calderone, M, ed., Abortion in the United States (New York: Hoeber and Harper, 1958).

2. Cooke, RE, et al., eds, The Terrible Choice: The Abortion Dilemma (New York: Bantam Books, 1968).

3. Lader, L, Abortion. Beacom Press, Boston, 1966, p.3.

4. Schwartz, RA: The Abortion Laws: A Severe Case of Resistance to Change. Ohio State Medical Journal, 67: 33-38, 1971.

5. Op. Cit., Lader, p. 176.

6. Niswander KR: Medical Abortion Practices in the United States. Case Western Reserve Law Review. 17: 402-423, 1965.

7. Nathanson BN: Aborting America, New York, Doubleday & Co., 1979, p. 193.

8. Clinton, Chelsea: Report on her Presentation on Abortion. National Television Networks, September, 2018.

9. Syska B, Hilgers TW, O'Hare D: An Objective Model of Estimating Criminal Abortions and Its Implications for Public Policy, In: Hilgers TW, Horan DJ, Mall D: New Perspectives on Human Abortion. University Publications of America, Frederick, Maryland, Chapter 13, pp. 164-181, 1981.

10. Hilgers TW, Horan DJ: Abortion and Social Justice. Sheed and Ward, New York, 1972.

11. Hilgers TW: *The Medical & Surgical Practice of* **NaProTECHNOLOGY.** Chapter on Prevention of Premature Labor. Pope Paul VI Institute Press, Omaha, NE 2004.

Chapter 4:

Maternal Mortality According to the Supreme Court

One of the foundational medical assumptions of *Roe v. Wade* was that first trimester abortion was **23.3 times safer** than **normal** or **ordinary** childbirth[1,2] and **it was promoted to the Court by the American College of Obstetricians & Gynecologists (ACOG).** They arrived at these numbers by taking the maternal mortality rate in the United States, which six years prior to *Roe v. Wade* was 28.0 per 100,000 live births and compared it to the maternal mortality rate in Hungary for *first trimester abortion* which was listed at 1.2 per 100,000 abortions. If you divide 28.0 by 1.2, the 23.3 times number is reached.[2] It should be noted that this was ultimately an "apples and oranges" comparison (live births from full-term pregnancy and up to 3–6 months postpartum versus first trimester abortions).

I have spent a lifetime trying to address these statistics and I must admit and even apologize for the fact that I have never been very successful at doing this. Having said that, however, I now know the mistake that I made. The United States Supreme Court accepted and put forth the notion that **"maternal mortality"** from **"ordinary"** or **"normal"** childbirth was extremely high compared to abortion and yet the maternal mortality rate from **"ordinary"** or **"normal"** childbirth is **actually zero!** If there is a maternal death related to childbirth or from pregnancy it is due to a ***catastrophic medical occurrence*** of some sort. It is far from "normal" or "ordinary."

Shortly after *Roe v. Wade* when I spent a lot of time with this data, I didn't see the terms "ordinary" or "normal" — even though they were there — I missed the point completely. The reason I did, however, was because I had in my mind a certain sense that the United States Supreme Court and the American College (ACOG) were trying to be honest with the American people and I just did not suspect deceptive or "fake" science like this. Now, I know differently. I know from the political struggles that are currently ongoing in the United States that lying and deceit have almost become a way of life. While many at the time of *Roe v. Wade* were up in arms because of this

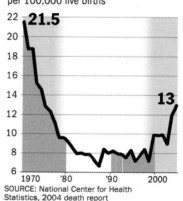

Maternal deaths

Women are dying from childbirth at the highest rate in decades, according to recent government figures.

Maternal mortality,
per 100,000 live births

SOURCE: National Center for Health Statistics, 2004 death report

THE ASSOCIATED PRESS

Figure 4-1: Increasing rate of maternal mortality in the U.S.

high rate of maternal mortality associated with "ordinary" or "normal" childbirth, there hasn't been much said since that time. It was used at a particular moment in time to persuade the Court to a particular point of view in favor of abortion.

In the early part of the 21st century, reports were beginning to be published that the maternal mortality rate was starting to increase again after it had dropped to an all-time low in the 1990s **(Figure 4-1)**. In 2017, data for the maternal mortality in the United States from 1999 until 2013 was published citing data from the Center for Disease Control & Prevention. In this case, the maternal mortality rate in the United States had reached 22 per 100,000 **(Figure 4-2)**. So, if you were to take the maternal mortality rate *without* nationalized abortion in

1972 (the figure that was known and available for 1971 and 1972 was 18.8 per 100,000) and compare it to the data in 2013, *with* a nationalized abortion program in the United States, this rate had actually increased. In other words, the maternal mortality rate *with* legalized abortion had **increased** over and above what occurred in 1971 and 1972 (Table 4-1). And yet, there is no outcry from those people who promoted abortion as there was in the early 1970s. There is no outcry from the American College of Obstetricians and Gynecologists as there was with their *Amicus* brief to the United States Supreme Court which was **submitted without a vote of their membership or their Board of Directors.** In addition, there's no outcry from anybody who listed their name on that *Amicus* brief.

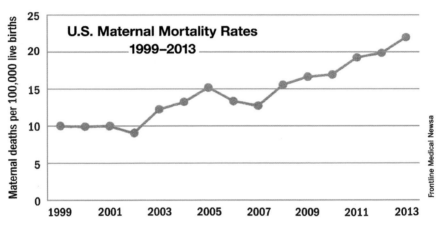

Figure 4-2: United States maternal mortality data, 1999–2013, U.S. Centers for Disease Control and Prevention as cited in Ob. Gyn. News, January, 2017.

This raises a significant question; and that question is "Do these people really care?" More and more, it begins to appear that they do not care about the women but they continue to care about winning their argument even if the data does not support it.

While one could argue this approach was an honest attempt to give context to these issues even though it is **not accurate;** however, it is more likely that it was placed before the Court without medical review in order to **deceive** the Court and the culture!

TABLE 4-1

UNITED STATES MATERNAL
MORTALITY RATE, 1960–1978[1]

Year	Rate	Year	Rate
1960	37.1	1969	22.2
1961	36.9	1970	21.5
1962	35.2	1971	18.8
1963	35.8	1972	18.8
1964	33.3	1973	15.2
1965	31.6	1974	14.6
1966	29.1	1975	12.8
1967	28.0	1976	12.3
1968	24.5	1977	11.2
		1978 (est.)	9.9

2013 = 22.0[2]

1. Data from: Monthly Vital Statistics Report. Provisional Statistics. Annual Summary for the United States, 1978, U.S. Dept. HEW, Office of Health Research, Statistics ad Technology, National Center for Health Statistics. 27:9, 1979.
2. Data from CDC for 2013 (from CDC, 2017).

In many ways, this argument got worse as *Roe v. Wade* and *Doe v. Bolton* was presented. As Blackmun's decision unfolded, he eventually said that the "mortality in abortion is less than mortality in *normal childbirth*" and that it was **"established medical fact."**[2] Nothing could be further from the truth and yet it was presented as scientific fact.

If this was stated by the U.S. Supreme Court *only* then one could argue that they did not have adequate expertise in this area to properly assess this. But this data was submitted to the Court with its calculation by the American College of Obstetricians and Gynecologists and that makes it a calculation by a professional organization who clearly should know better! **It was clearly a number that was spun to meet the needs of their pro-abortion lobby.** It was a calculation that was **deceptive** at the best and **fake** at the least!

CHAPTER 4
REFERENCES AND FOOTNOTES

1. From: *Amicus Curiae* Brief filed on behalf of the American College of Obstetricians & Gynecologists, the American Medical Women's Association, the American Psychiatric Association, the New York Academy of Medicine, Medical School Deans and Professors, and certain individual physicians, in *Doe v. Bolton*, 410 U.S. 179 (1973).

   In the summer of 1971, the American College of Obstetricians and Gynecologists filed an *Amicus Curiae* brief before the United States Supreme Court as an intervention in the constitutionality hearing of the Georgia abortion statute (*Doe v. Bolton*). In this brief, the claim was made that "the medical procedure of induced abortion ... is potentially 23.3 times as safe as the process of going through ordinary childbirth."

2. *Roe v. Wade*, 410 U.S. 113 (1973) and *Doe v. Bolton*, 410 U.S. 173 (1973).

   Later in 1973, when the United States Supreme Court issued its now historic decision regarding abortion, it accepted as **"established medical fact"** the contention that in the first three months of pregnancy "mortality in abortion is less than mortality in normal childbirth."

Chapter 5

The "New Embryological Data" of the Supreme Court

Justice Blackmun suggests that "substantial problems for a precise definition of this view (meaning that individual life begins at the moment of conception) are opposed, however, by **new embryological data** (emphasis applied) that purport to indicate that conception is a 'process' over time rather than an 'event,' and by new medical techniques such as menstrual extraction, the 'morning after pill,' implantation of embryos, artificial insemination and even artificial wombs."[1]

In looking at the question of the presence of "new embryological data ... conception as a 'process' over time, rather than an event," Blackmun uses the following citations that include five law reviews (Journal of Family Law, UCLA, Oregon and Michigan Law Reviews and the University of Illinois Law Forum). In addition, he cites two books which are speculative ventures without scientific foundation written by lay authors as opposed to trained embryological scientists. This includes Gordon Rattray Taylor's book, *"The Biological Time*

Bomb"[2] published in 1968, and Isaac Rosenfeld's book, *"The Second Genesis"*[3] published in 1969. A positive conclusion relative to these two books that would give any credence to the notion that there is "new embryological data" to which Blackmun refers is not possible because it does not exist except in the minds of these amateurs.

In Roderic Gorney's (a psychiatrist) 1968 Law Review article entitled, *"The New Biology and the Future of Man,"*[4] he does give us a hint as to what Blackmun might be referring to. He says the following:

> "Aristotle believed life begins at the time of 'quickening,' the first movement of the baby in the womb — and this is the Jewish position today. Catholic doctrine maintains that life begins at conception. One Protestant view concurs. Another holds that while life begins at conception, the person begins only at birth. **One could also say that life is present in the sperm and egg and the cells that give rise to them, so that while there may be a moment when a life ends, no life has begun in three billion years."**

This begins to appear significant until one traces it back to an article in 1963 from *The Eugenics Review* by Glanville Williams[5] who, at the time, was the President of the Abortion Law Reform Association of England. The article was the manuscript of his talk that was given at the annual meeting of that Association in 1964. Williams was in the midst of a debate with Norman St John-Stevas, a member of the British Parliament who was pro-life. St John-Stevas said that the right to life begins at conception, "But when one looks more closely, one finds that this assertion is supported by the religious argument, which runs as follows. Formerly, it was thought that some qualitative change took place in the embryo during its development; this qualitative change was supposed to be accompanied by the infusion of the soul:

> "Today, and indeed for a very considerable period, it has been accepted by biologists that there is no qualitative difference between the embryo at the moment of conception and at the moment of quickening. Life is fully present at the moment of conception. It follows that if

there be a soul, it too must be present from the time of conception."

Williams goes on to say that, "This looks like a compelling argument, until one begins to apply the same type of reasoning to this supposed moment of conception. What is the moment of conception? It is not a moment at all. Like the development of the embryo, it is a process. I *believe* that the *latest biological account* is as follows: The sperm meets and joins with the ovum. Two structures called asters appear, and a spindle forms between them. The chromosomes from the egg nucleus and the sperm nucleus collect around the equator of the spindle before dividing longitudinally into halves which move towards the asters, forming two daughter nuclei. Finally the cytoplasm of the egg cell divides and two new cells result."

He goes on to say that, "Now Dr. St. John Steves says that 'life is fully present from the moment of conception.' So it is, but life is just as fully present **before** the moment of conception: And the 'moment of conception' *is a figment of the imagination, since conception like everything else is a process which takes time. The argument that life begins with conception is just as unbiological as the notion that life begins sometime after conception.*

"To this the reply will certainly be made: We are not speaking just of life, but of *human* life." Williams goes on to say that, "Here, I think we have arrived *at the real question;* and when one asks it in this form, it becomes evident that the answer depends upon a **somewhat arbitrary choice of language.** Do you wish to regard the microscopic fertilized ovum as a human being? You can if you want to, and if there were no *social consequences* of doing so, there might be no reason why you should not. But there are most important *social arguments* for *not* adopting this language.[6] Moreover, if you look at actual beliefs and behavior, you will find almost unanimous rejection of it.

"*The law* does not look upon a natural miscarriage as the death of a human being. A foetus that is spontaneously aborted before the end of the 7th month can be buried in the back garden, or put in a hospital incinerator. No statutory notice of birth need be given. No religious community performs a funeral service for an aborted embryo. No one attempts to baptize the microscopic ovum. A Roman Catholic priest will, if called upon, attempt to baptize an aborted foetus that has attained such a size that it can be recognized as such; but Catholic doctrine is still not finally settled on the time of entry of the soul, so Catholics do not recognize it as certain that baptism can be effective if it is administered too early in the development of the foetus. If the baptism is administered, therefore, it is just to be on the safe side.

"Only in our own time have embryologists discovered the immense rate of natural wastage of the foetus. One in three and possibly one in two of all fertilized human ova are destined to be lost by spontaneous abortion or re-absorption (see chapter ten).[6] We do not regard these natural miscarriages as equivalent to the *death of a child* — even the mother herself does not do so. She regards it only as the loss of a potential child.

"At least in the very early stages of pregnancy, we do not consider that a *human being* is in existence, but only a *potential human being*. It is true that law and religious belief generally look upon induced abortion as wrongful, but this hardly reflects *popular* attitudes (emphasis applied). Neither the law nor the Church has succeeded in persuading the ordinary woman that it is wrongful for her to endeavor to terminate a pregnancy in the early stages, if having a child would be a serious burden to her."

So it appears that Glanville Williams is the source of most of this and not anything that's in these law review articles or the books of Rattray Taylor's and/or Rosenfeld. To cite these two authors, even though they do not support Blackmun's analysis, he chose to do this most likely because they would be safe since Glanville Williams was known to be very pro-abortion. If, however, Blackmun believed these previous seven paragraphs as the main argument in favor of abortion, why was it not used as his argument in *Roe?* Was it because Glanville Williams was problematic with his openly pro-abortion position — an advocate if you will — and citing Williams would be too revealing of his bias?

This juxtaposition of *"social consequences"* which had important *"social arguments"* has become one of the most commonly-cited reasons for abortion. Basically, unborn life becomes irrelevant in this view and it can be destroyed at the whim of the social consequence. Ultimately, this rationale is **weak** but also reflects the unwillingness to respond in a positive way to these consequences. Of course, once abortion is legal and available "on demand," the "easy way out" has become the solution. What has been missed is how few of these consequences are really

FIGURE 5-1

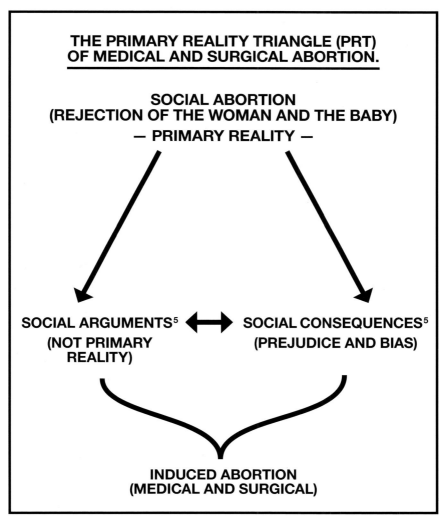

Figure 5-1: The Primary Reality Triangle of medical and surgical abortion.

solved and how many are harmed by a surgical/medical approach that is aimed at emptying the uterus. There are better solutions that are so easy to bypass for the lack of any positive energy to become involved in being a part of the solution. **Is this really the best we have to offer?** Ultimately, we accept *"social abortion,"* the rejection of the woman who is pregnant and distressed (see glossary for further definition of "social abortion") by submitting her to a vicious and violent solution to her *"social consequences" (The Reality Triangle of Medical and Surgical Abortion,* see Figure 5-1) through various *social arguments* (not primary reality).

In fact, it's interesting in reading **Rattray Taylor** that after all the nuance of trying to establish this futuristic thought in human biology, he says that:

> "There is no doubt a danger that a general realization of the mechanical nature of living systems — however exquisitely organized they be — may lead to a **cheapening of life** and a tendency to regard it as expendable and unworthy of respect. How serious this danger will depend, I suppose, on how far the general level of intelligence has been improved and how far educationists have managed to tackle the problem of orienting pupils to the realities of existence instead of stuffing them with facts and techniques. **For (need it be said) no such disrespect for life is justified or justifiable"** (emphasis applied).

So even Rattray Taylor points out the potential problems for the cheapening of life with these approaches, but this was completely *selected out* of the analysis that Blackmun did, and, of course, we've been seeing the "cheapening of life" now after more than 60 million abortions.

In effect, this argument falls upon the notion that the sperm cell and the egg cell are "alive." This is, of course, quite true just like a liver cell or a brain cell or a pulmonary cell are generally alive. However, they are all nonexistent until the egg and sperm unite and then progress forward in their growth and development as this new human person. The *natural tendency of the ovum* once it has been released from the ovary is to *die within 12–24 hours after ovulation. So its life is short-lived.* The *same thing is true for the sperm.* Once released from the man's body, they do have a potential survivability of 8 or 9 days, *but their fertilizing capability only lasts 3 to 5 days.* If they do not penetrate an ovum, all of the sperm die within a relatively short period and do **not** have life "fully present" as the zygote would have. If one of the sperm enters the ovum, then the new cell, which is now a *zygote*, has a different compliment of genes and chromosomes unique to this individual human person, and will continue to grow with life "fully present" as that unique person. But the zygote is neither the ovum nor is it the sperm. Of course, life in general terms has existed on this planet for millions and millions of years, but nobody's ever been talking about that in this debate (unless trying to persuade us to be pro-abortion with invalid arguments). What has been talked about is the individual life that comes into existence at the moment that a human being is conceived (the union of the egg and the sperm). To think that that is not a true "moment" because it takes some time, is also interesting in itself because the word "moment" does not mean instantaneous. Most people would say that it probably takes 1 to 30 minutes for all of this to take place, but it's still considered a moment or the moment of conception.

Maureen Condic, PhD, an Associate Professor of Neurobiology and Anatomy at the University of Utah School of Medicine, wrote one of the most scientifically definitive papers on this subject in 2008 (although this knowledge was also known in 1973 before the release of *Roe* and *Doe).*

> "The **zygote** [emphasis added] forms immediately upon sperm-egg fusion. Factors from the sperm initiate completion of meiosis II in the maternally-derived nucleus. Within 1-3 minutes, changes in cellular calcium initiate the cortical reaction of the zygote, making the cell refractory to fusion with other sperm. Within 30 minutes, meiosis II is complete, establishing the final diploid genome of the zygote. Sperm binding sites in the zona pellucida are destroyed.[7]

So it's very interesting how they've twisted the language to make us believe that this is a new biology. The *denial of biological realism*, **the**

idea that every human being on this earth was in existence three billion years ago is just ludicrous![1] We all began at the moment that our parents' sperm and ovum united. And that's actually what makes us unique from all other people in the world. There is a unique genotype that has been placed together with that union and that genotype allows for the phenotype of this new person to be expressed; and it should be stated strongly that the genotype is everything to this new human person. This individual was never present before this occurred and is only present during the lifetime of this new person until natural death (unless some interruption of that life occurs). This can occur as a result of an accident, a disease of some sort or because somebody purposely ends that life — which is what happens in induced abortion. So there will be more commentary on this later and will be more easily understood.

Blackmun pushes on: "In areas other than criminal abortion, the law has been reluctant to endorse any theory that life, as we recognize it, begins before live birth or to accord legal rights to the unborn except in narrowly-defined situations and except when the rights are contingent upon live birth."[2] And ultimately comes to the conclusion that "In short, **the unborn have never been recognized in the law as persons in the *whole sense*"** (emphasis applied). What Blackmun says in *Roe* is the same mistake made in *Dred Scott.*

I was interviewed by a reporter from the Washington Post several years ago and he took the position of Glanville Williams. He asked me what I would do with "the millions of human lives (sperm) that are deposited in the vagina at the time of intercourse and subsequently die. What would you do for all of these lives?" In response I told him the following: *"You may be a grown-up sperm, but I am not!"* (See *epilogue.*) Enough said for now.

CHAPTER 5
REFERENCES AND FOOTNOTES

1. *Roe v. Wade*, 314F. Supp. 1217, United States Supreme Court, No. 70-18, January 22, 1973.

2. Taylor GR: The Biological Time Bomb, World Publishing Co., New York and Cleveland, 1968, p. 32.

3. Rosenfeld A: The Second Genesis: The Coming Control of Life. Prentice-Hall, Englewood Cliffs, New Jersey, 1969.

4. Gorney R: The New Biology and the Future of Man, 15 UCLA L. Rev. 273, 1968, p. 311

5. Williams G: The Legalization of Medical Abortion. The Eugenics Review, April 1964.

6. This notion of a high rate of "natural wastage" of the "foetus" has been promoted for several years by those who favor abortion, but the research behind this supposition is seriously deficient. This is discussed in further detail in Chapter Ten.

7. Condic M: When Does Human Life Begin? A Scientific Perspective. White Paper, The Westchester Institute for Ethics and the Human Person, Thornwood, NY, 2008, p. 17.

Chapter 6:

When Does Human Life Begin?

In the process of producing and issuing *Roe v. Wade* and *Doe v. Bolton*, ***Blackmun attempted to re-write the facts of human biology without any scientific substance to his claims.*** This is perhaps one of the most egregious attempts by a major authoritative body to re-write science without any scientific validation. ***Human life begins at the moment of conception — at that moment when sperm and egg unite — and this is a scientific fact!*** It is at this moment that a totally new and unique individual, never before in existence, never again to be duplicated, comes to be.

This origin of new human life is strongly supported by the testimony of the **scientific community** (which was completely ignored and rejected in *Roe* and *Doe*) most of whom have spent their lives studying early human development (in chronological order):

Quimby, I.N.: Introduction to Medical Jurisprudence. Address delivered by the Chairman of the section on medical jurisprudence at the 38th Annual Meeting of the A.M.A., June 10, 1887.

JAMA 9:161-166, August 6, 1887.

> "… The entire organized human body may be considered to be made up of congeries of cells, each set having its own life and appropriate functions. From these cells the embryo and fetus is developed. *This is a truth so well settled that no well-informed physician would care to deny it* (emphasis applied). So we … assert most positively that **the life of the foetus** *commences at the moment of conception* …"

Heisler, JC: A Textbook of Embryology for Students of Medicine. W. B. Saunders, Philadelphia and London, 1901, 2nd Edition, 1901, p. 38.

> "**Fertilization** is that … union of spermatozoa and egg-cell which initiates the phenomenon *resulting in the formation of a new individual.*"

Edgar JC: The Practice of Obstetrics, 3rd Edition, P. Blakiston's Son and Co., Philadelphia, 1908.

> "When this occurs (the ovum and spermatozoa come together), *the woman conceives* and *enters into the period of pregnancy or gestation.*"

McMurrich, JM: The Development of the Human Body: A Manual of Human Embryology. P. Blakiston's Sons & Company, Philadelphia, 7th Edition, 1923, p. 31.

> "…As a matter of fact, such a restoration (of cells) *occurs at the very beginning of the development of each individual,* being brought about by *the union of a spermatozoa with an ovum.*"

Gilbert, M.S.: Biography of the Unborn. Williams and Wilkins Company, Baltimore, 1938, pp. 2 and 5.

"Not until the 19ᵗʰ century did men finally realize that the union of the sperm with the egg creates a new human being. Life begins for each of us at an unfelt, unknown and unhonored instant when a minute wriggling sperm plunges headlong into a mature ovum or egg … It is at this moment of fusion of the ovum and the sperm (a process called fertilization) that a new human being is created."

Hamilton, WJ, et al: Human Embryology (Prenatal Development of Form and Function). Williams and Wilkins Company, Baltimore, 1945, p. 1.

"There are no essential differences between prenatal and postnatal development; the former is more rapid and results in more striking changes in shape and proportions, but in both the basic mechanisms are very similar if not identical."

Dodds, GD: The Essentials of Human Embryology. J. Wiley and Sons, Inc. New York, 1946, 3rd Edition, p. 2.

"This fertilized egg is the beginning of a new individual."

Patten, B.M: Human Embryology. 2nd Edition. The Blackiston Company, Inc., Toronto and New York, 1953, p. 52.

"There is perhaps no phenomenon in the field of biology that touches so many fundamental questions as the union of the germ cells in the act of fertilization; in this supreme event, all the strands of the webs of two lives are gathered in one knot, from which they diverge again and are rewoven in a new individual life-history… *The elements that unite are single cells, each on the point of death; but by their union a[n] … individual is formed…"*

Hartman, Carl G: Science and the Safe Period: A Compendium of Human Reproduction. The Williams & Wilkins Co., Baltimore, 1962, pp. 95-96. (Dr. Hartman was a research consultant for the

Margaret Sanger Research Bureau **at the time his book was written.)**

> "After the sperm has entered the vitellus, as seen in the Blandau movie and photographed also by Austin with the phase contrast microscope (Austin & Braden, 1952, 1956), the sperm, had undergone liquefaction and the chromosomal material reconstitutes itself into a nucleus and a number of nucleoli. In the meantime, under the stimulus of the entering sperm, the ovum casts off the second polar body and 23 (reduced number) of chromosomes, while the 23 chromosomes left in the egg (the female contribution to the offspring) form the female pronucleus. The pronuclei approach each other and fuse. The combined chromosomes (now 46; 23 from each parent) arrange themselves in an equatorial plate, they split lengthwise, the cells divide into 2 cells, *and **the new individual may be said to have begun its development.**"

Flanagan, Geraldine Lux: The First Nine Months of Life. Simon & Schuster, New York, NY, 1962, pp. 25, 26.

> "When the sperm nucleus reaches the egg nucleus, these two lie side by side as their content is combined. In this half-hour, an immeasurable number of traits of the new baby are decided within the pin-point egg. These include the features of the human species and also the individual trademarks such as male or female sex; the color of eyes, hair and skin; the configuration of face and body; the tendency to be tall or short, fat or lean, ruggedly healthy or prone to some diseases; and undoubtedly also the tendency to certain qualities of temperament and intelligence. With so many genes joined when the parent cells unite, there is obviously vast possibility for new variety of the existing family patterns. ***Each new baby is a unique individual, never entirely like either parent or any ancestor.***

"As the synthesis of the two different parent nuclei is completed within the single egg, two new nuclei arise. The genetic make-up of these two nuclei differs from that of either parent: It is a blend of both. *That moment, when the two new nuclei form and the now fertilized egg divides in two is the beginning of the life of a new individual. This is zero hour of day one.*"

Dr. George W. Corner, the former Director of the Department of Embryology at the Carnegie Institution of Washington and Professor Emeritus of Embryology at Johns Hopkins University, said about the Flanagan book (1962) the following:

"Considering that every human being was once an embryo, and that the majority of adults become parents, it is rather remarkable but the story of our first nine months remains for most people one of nature's mysteries, or even lies under a taboo as if it were somehow improper to have been an embryo.

"Scientists who spend their lives studying embryology are inevitably impressed by the wonder and beauty of human development as well as by its biologic complexity, but their research articles and textbooks are technical, illustrated with complicated diagrams and drawings …

"Mrs. Flanagan combines excellent preparation in biology and a clever pen, but the young mother's interest in the process of child-bearing, she has made the story clear, without excessive detail. **Yet, its accuracy is attested to by experienced embryologists.** She has chosen illustrations worthy of her text. Many come from the great archive of the Department of Embryology at the Carnegie Institution of Washington. Originally intended solely for research, but made with a keen eye for the esthetic as well as the scientific aspects of the subject, these photographs clarify in a spectacular way the changing form of the human embryo …"

This is from the Forward of the Second Edition of "The First Nine Months of Life." Mrs. Flanagan writes that, "In the preparation of the manuscript numerous friends and acquaintances have helped immeasurably in showing their interest in giving needed advice. Of those who read the manuscript for clarity and accuracy, I would like to mention, most especially, **Dr. George W. Corner** who kindly reviewed the entire text. Also **Dr. Davenport Hooker** who reviewed the text, in particular the sections on the development of motion."

Davies, J: Human Developmental Anatomy, Ronald Press Co. New York, 1963, p. 3.

"Human development may be said to begin with the union of the male and female germ cells in the act of fertilization."

Guttmacher, AF, et al: Planning your Family. MacMillan Co., New York and London, 1964, p. 36.

After explaining the process of fertilization, he stated, *"Fertilization, then, has taken place; a baby has been conceived.* After conception occurs, the egg attaches itself to the wall of the womb where it grows nine months until the baby is ready to be born."

Arey, CB: Developmental Anatomy: A Textbook and Laboratory Manual of Embryology. W.B. Saunders Co., Philadelphia and London, 1965, p. 55.

The union of the male and female sex cell "definitely marks the beginning of a new individual."

Liley, H.M.I. Modern Motherhood. New York, Random House,

1967.

Noted pediatrician, Dr. H.M.I. Liley, in her book, Modern Motherhood stated, *"From the moment a baby is conceived, it bears the indelible stamp of a separate, distinct personality, an individual different from all other individuals."*

Gordon, Hymie: Genetical, Social and Medical Aspects of Abortion. South African Medical Journal, July 20, 1968, pp. 721-730. (Dr. Gordon, in 1973, was the Chief Geneticist at the Mayo Clinic and signed onto the Amicus Brief that presented the Court with opposition to abortion).

"... From the moment of fertilization, when the deoxyribonucleic acids from the spermatozoa and the ovum come together to form the zygote, the pattern of the individual's constitutional development is irrevocably determined; his future health, his future intellectual potential, even his future criminal proclivities are all dependent on the sequence of the purine and pyrimidine bases in the original set of DNA molecules of the unicellular individual. ... *It is at the moment of conception that the individual's capacity to respond to ... exogenous influences is established. ... It is a privilege to be allowed to protect and nurture it."*

Langman J: Medical Embryology. 2nd Edition, Williams and Wilkins & Co., Baltimore, 1969, p. 3.

"The development of a human being begins with fertilization."

Shettles, LB. JAMA 214:1895, December 7, 1970.

"By ... definition a new composite individual is started at the moment of fertilization."

Hellman, LM and Pritchard, JA: Williams Obstetrics 14th Edition, Appleton-Century-Cross Educational Division/Meredith Corporation, New York, NY, 1971, p. 122.

> *"In mammals, … the union of sperm and egg is requisite to the development of the normal adult. …"*

From: Blechschmidt, E: Human Being from the Very First (translated by Ernst J. Brehm). In: Hilgers TW, Horan DJ and Mall D: New Perspectives on Human Abortion. Aletheia Books, University Publications of America, Frederick, MD, 1981. (Work done 1930-1972.)

From the years "1930 to 1972, most especially at the Anatomical Institute of the University of Göttingen, West Germany," the embryologist, Professor E. Blechschmidt assembled the Blechschmidt Human-Embryological Documentation Collection. From that he made a number of striking and important observations:

> " … *The question regarding the point in the course of prenatal development at which it is licit to speak of a human being can be clearly answered, because today we know that each developmental stage of the human being is demonstrably a characteristically human one.* Already, on the basis of the well-known chromosomes of human ova, the specificity of a human germ can no longer be doubted. Therefore, this principle applies today: ***A human being does not become a human being but rather is such from the instant of its fertilization. During the entire ontogenesis, no single break can be demonstrated, either in the sense of a leap from the lifeless to the live, or of a transition from the vegetative to the instinctive or to characteristically human behavior.*** It may be considered today a fundamental law of human ontogenesis that not only

human specificity, but also the individual specificity of each human being remains preserved from fertilization to death, and that only the appearance of the individual being changes in the course of its ontogenesis."

"What we term the ontogenesis of a human being begins with fertilization because the fertilized ovum is already a form of man."

"The young human ovum measures about 0.1 mm in diameter and weighs only 0.0004 mg. The major part of its volume consists of water. For this reason, very young human embryos are as a rule transparent and hardly perceptible. Nevertheless, the morphological possibility of distinguishing the human ovum from other living ova indicates that its activity, too, is a special one from the very first."

THE SINGLE MOST IMPORTANT HUMAN CELL (SMIHC)

The above-cited scientific work which was all available to the Court pre-*Roe*, has continued to advance over these last several decades. The three-dimensional ultrasound now shows clearly the human parameters of the human child *in utero* (see **Chapter 7**). Four-dimensional ultrasound shows the early fetus moving in its mother's womb (see: the prepared video that is available at no cost at ***www.knowreality.us***). The relatively new science of DNA typing can distinguish the unique characteristics of that human literally from the moment of conception. *In vitro* fertilization, while it dehumanizes the early human person because it is such a highly abortive technology, does prove without a doubt that a new individual life begins when the sperm and egg unite. No IVF babies have been born where this event has been skipped over. The *zygote* is an extraordinary cell with capabilities beyond all other cells in the human body because it is programmed to be so absolutely significant to the ongoing growth and development of the new human person. Blackmun likes to refer to this as *potential human life* which he does over and over and over again in *Roe*.[1] And yet, there's nothing "potential" about it. It is actual human life! **It is human life with potential!**[3]

The *human zygote* is the *single most important human cell* (SMIHC)! *It is a cell that* **precedes** *all stem cells.* It is the **originating cell** of each individual human life. It has extraordinary capabilities. **We all started with the *SMIHC* and if our lives have any value now, the *SMIHC* surely had value then.**

Many people like to say that this is a "belief." By putting it into the context of a belief, it is made to seem like one has to have a special faith to be able to see the unborn in its reality. An yet, none of that is true. This is a scientific observation — objective, species specific, reproducible and enlightened. We have made *a gross error* as a nation and a culture in denying it.

After ignoring and purposely rejecting 400 years of scientific progress in our understanding of the growth and development of the human being *in utero*, Blackmun says that he was influenced by the development of "new embryological data …" and that conception is "a process over time, rather than an event."[2] He used seven citations to justify this. One would presume that they were all from credible scientific sources. But five of them were from law reviews and two of them were from lay science writers. **None of them were credible scientific sources. He accepted a small minority view of life** (similar in context to the flat-earth society) **and actually rejected the consensus!**

CHAPTER 6
REFERENCES AND FOOTNOTES

1. *Roe v. Wade,* 314F. Supp. 1217, United States Supreme Court, No. 70-18, January 22, 1973, p. 35, 38, 44, 46-47, 48, 49.

2. Op Cit, *Roe v. Wade*, p. 45.

 * The references for the location of the quotes in this chapter are included in the text of the chapter.

3. Joyce RE and Joyce MR: Let Us Be Born, The Inhumanity of Abortion. Franciscan World Press. Chicago, 1970, p. 23.

Chapter 7

A Picture Dictionary of Human Life in the Womb (circa 1973)

(A video of this chapter — with motion pictures — is available at no cost at ***www.knowreality.us***.)

THE MOMENT OF CONCEPTION

The egg (ovum) and sperm both have a limited life spam. The ovum, once released, dies 12–24 hours later. The sperm lives for 8–9 days, but it is capable of fertilizing the ovum for a maximum of only 3–5 days.

The supreme court (Blackmun) led us to think that we are just a grown up sperm or a grown up egg.

The sperm in this photo (7B) is about to enter the ovum.

7A. 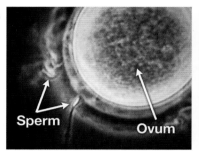 7B.

7C.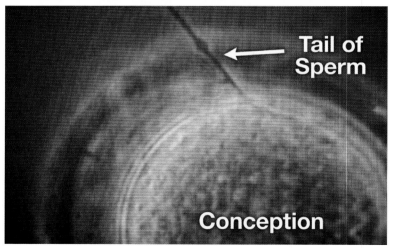

The tail of the sperm is visible but outside the ovum (7C). The head of the sperm that contains 50% of the chromosomal compliment of the new human person is now inside the ovum (7C) and in 15–30 minutes it joins with the other 50% of the chromosomes contributed by the ovum. This is the *moment of conception* with an average lifespan of about 75 years for males and 81 years for females.

FIGURES 7-1 A, B, & C

FIGURE 7-2A

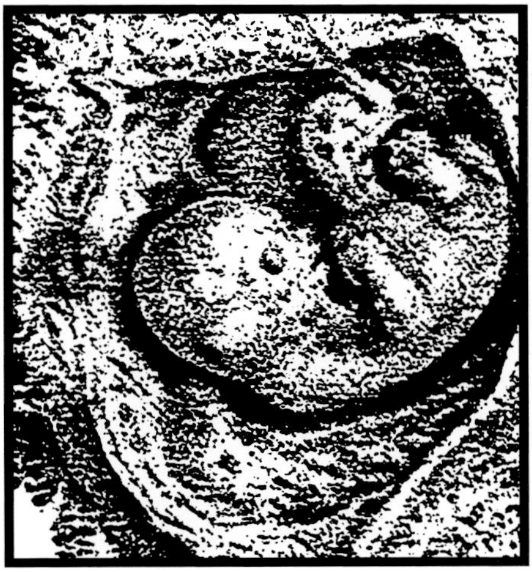

FIGURE 7-2B

HUNTER
1774
6-7 WEEKS

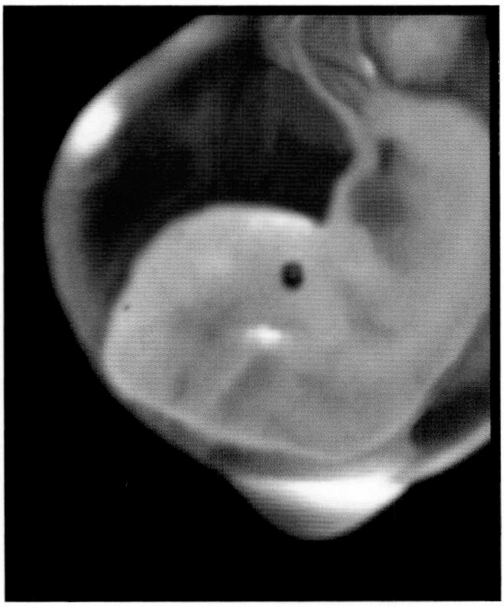

HILGERS
1970s
6-7 WEEKS

Figure 7-2A & 7-2B: On the left is a copy of the original drawing of the embryo at 6–7 weeks published by Dr. William Hunter, the Queen's physician in 1774. On the right is an actual color photo of an embryo at the comparable size taken in the 1970s (Photo: Thomas W. Hilgers, MD).

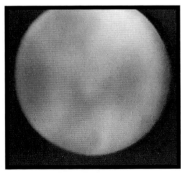

Figure 7-2C: A color picture of the embryo's heart at 28 days post-conception. Live action of this heartbeat is on the video that is freely available at ***www.knowreality.us***. The embryo's heartbeat is 120 beats per minute, contrasted to the maternal heartbeat, which averages 72 beats per minute.

FIGURE 7-2C

FIGURE 7-3

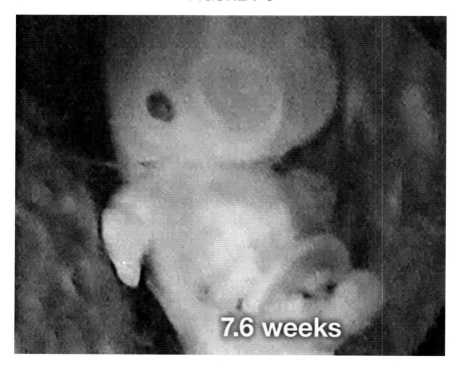

7.6 WEEKS

Figure 7-3: 7.6 weeks gestational age and 5.6 weeks fetal age by direct color photography. The arms and legs can now be seen, the large reddish area in the mid-torso is the heart. The heart is already beating! (Photo: Thomas W. Hilgers, MD).

FIGURE 7-4

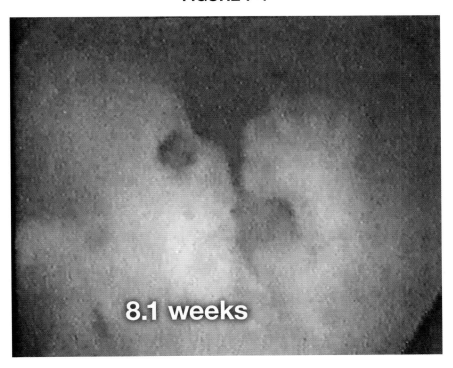

8.1 WEEKS

Figure 7-4: Profile of fetus at 8.1 weeks gestational age, 6.1 fetal age. The eye, right hand, profile with the nose and lips visible are shown. (Photo: Thomas W. Hilgers, MD).

FIGURES 7-5A AND 7-5B

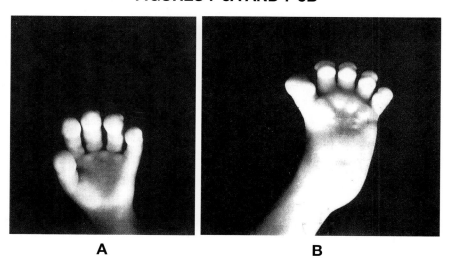

A   **B**

Figure 7-5A and B: The fingers and thumb of the left hand (A) at the beginning of the seventh week. Fingerprints are forming. Large and small toes of the left foot at the beginning of the seventh week (B).

FIGURE 7-6

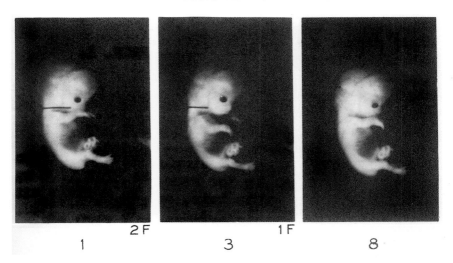

2 F   1 F

1   3   8

Figure 7-6: Davenport Hooker's work showing movement at 8.5 week gestational age and 6.5 weeks fetal age. A horsehair is used to stroke the right cheek of the embryo in Figure 1, the right arm drops down in Figure 3 and returns to its starting position in Figure 8.

FIGURE 7-7

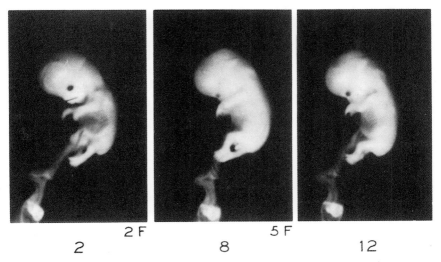

2 F   5 F

2   8   12

Figure 7-7: Response to tactile stimulation of the face. Probable menstrual age or gestational age 8.5 weeks and 6.5 weeks fetal age. In the first photo (No. 2), the left cheek is stroked and the head first moves to the left, and in Figure 8 moves back to the right. In Figure 12, the embryo resumes in starting position.

[From: Actual motion pictures taken by Davenport Hooker, PhD, published 1939.]

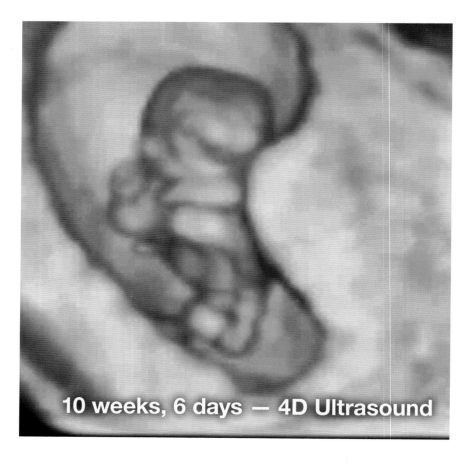

10 WEEKS, 6 DAYS

Figure 7-8: A 3 and 4 dimensional ultrasound of the fetus at 10 weeks 6 days gestational age (8 weeks 6 days fetal age) (Saint Paul VI Institute Reproductive ultrasound Center). A 4 dimension ultrasound of the same baby with its extraordinary level of movement is included in the free video.

FIGURE 7-9

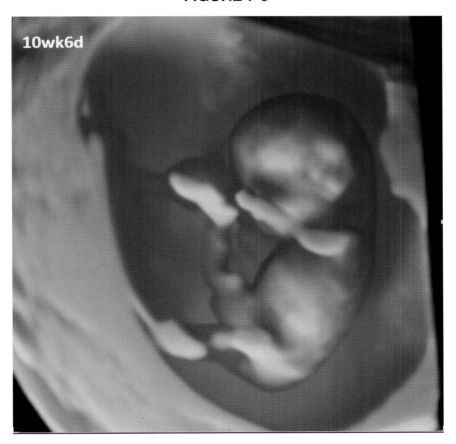

Figure 7-9: 3 dimensional ultrasound of fetus at gestational age of 10 weeks 6 days and 8 weeks, 6 days fetal age. (Saint Paul VI Institute Reproductive ultrasound Center). An ultrasound smoothing effect has been used to produce an even more realistic picture.

10 WEEKS, 6 DAYS

FIGURE 7-10

11 WEEKS
RESPONSE TO EXTERNAL STIMULATION

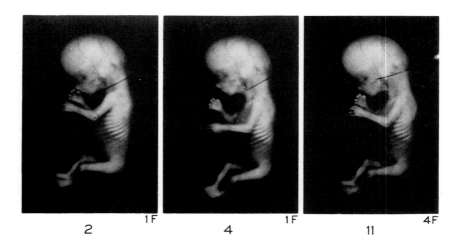

2   1 F   1 F   4 F
                 4   11

Figure 7-10: Fetus at a probable gestational age of 11 weeks (9 weeks fetal age) responding to tactile stimulation of the face with a hair, No. 2: Backward movement of both arms in response to stimulation, No. 4: Caudal movement of both forearms and hands more pronounced on the ipsilateral than on the contralateral side but without extension of the elbow. No. 11: Return to normal fetal posture of the upper extremities. The time between frames 2 and 4 is 0.125 seconds and between 4 and 11 is 1.06 seconds. (From: Hooker D: A Preliminary Atlas of Early Human Fetal Activity. From: The Ladd Laboratory of the Department of Anatomy, University of Pittsburgh School of Medicine. Published by the author, Davenport Hooker, PhD, p. 34 - Plate No. 26, 1939).

FIGURE 7-11
FROM HUNTER, 1774

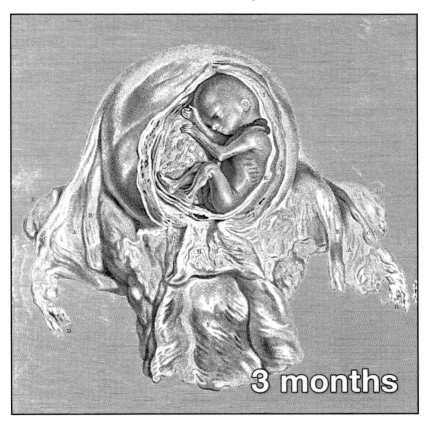

3 MONTHS
HUNTER: 1774

FIGURE 7-12: 3D ULTRASOUND AT 16 WEEKS, 6 DAYS, APPEARS TO BE SMILING

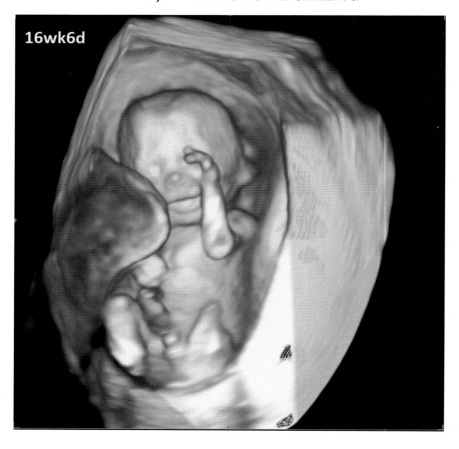

**16 WEEKS
6 DAYS
GESTATIONAL AGE**

**FIGURE 7-13: 3D ULTRASOUND AT 16 WEEKS, 6 DAYS
SAME VIEW AS IN FIG. 7-12 WITH
ADDITION OF "SMOOTHING" TECHNIQUES
AVAILABLE ON ULTRASOUND.**

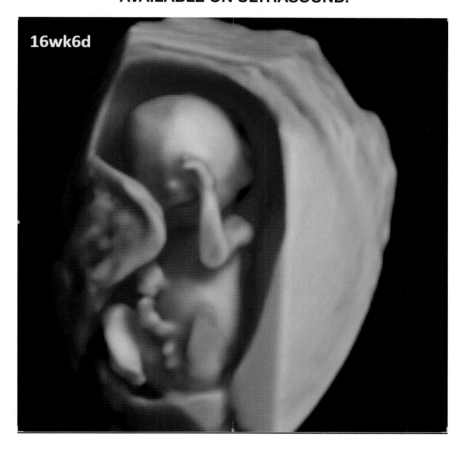

16wk6d

**16 WEEKS
6 DAYS
GESTATIONAL AGE**

FIGURE 7-14: MOUTH WIDE OPEN, 3D ULTRASOUND
AT 16 WEEKS GESTATIONAL AGE

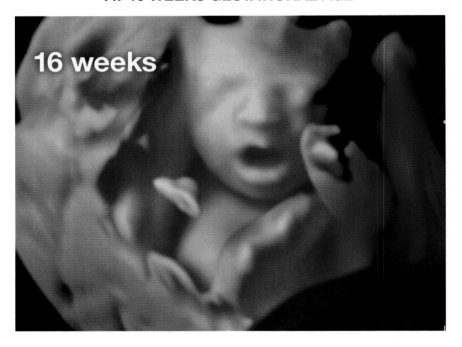

MOUTH OPEN

FIGURE 7-15:

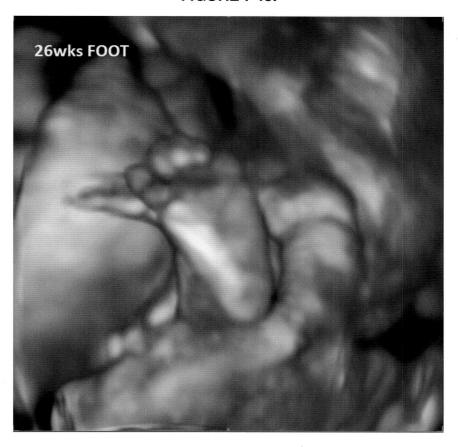

**3D ULTRASOUND
FOOT AND TOES — 26 WEEKS
GESTATIONAL AGE**

FIGURE 7-16: 3D ULTRASOUND AT 26 WEEKS, RIGHT HAND ON THE BROW

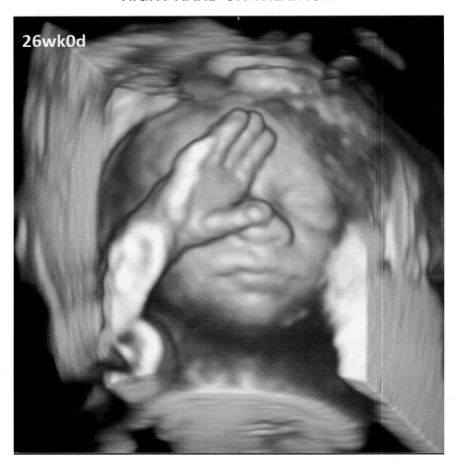

26 WEEKS
GESTATIONAL AGE

FIGURE 7-17: 3D ULTRASOUND AT
26 WEEKS WITH MOUTH WIDE OPEN

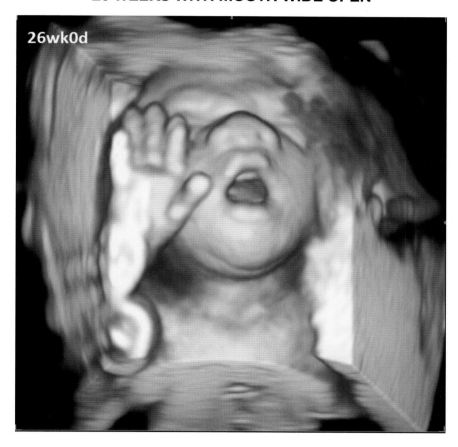

MOUTH OPEN — 26 WEEKS
GESTATIONAL AGE

FIGURE 7-18: 3D ULTRASOUND OF FACIAL FEATURES AT 26 WEEKS (USING "SMOOTHING" TECHNIQUES AVAILABLE ON 3D ULTRASOUND). FROM ST. PAUL VI INSTITUTE REPRODUCTIVE ULTRASOUND CENTER, 2019.

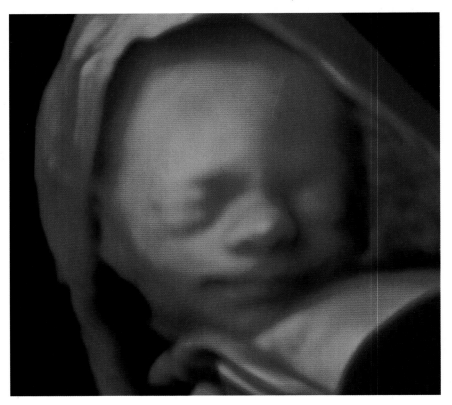

26 WEEKS GESTATIONAL AGE

FIGURE 7-19: FROM HUNTER, 1774 AT 6 MONTHS

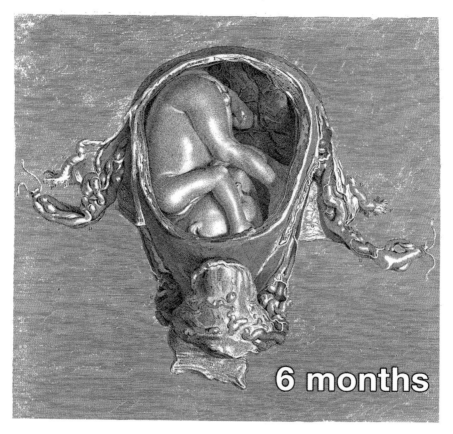

6 MONTHS
HUNTER, 1774

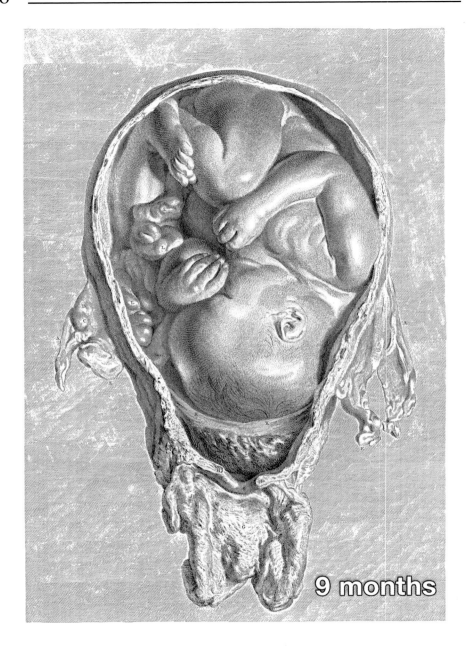

FIGURE 7-20
9 MONTHS
HUNTER: 1774

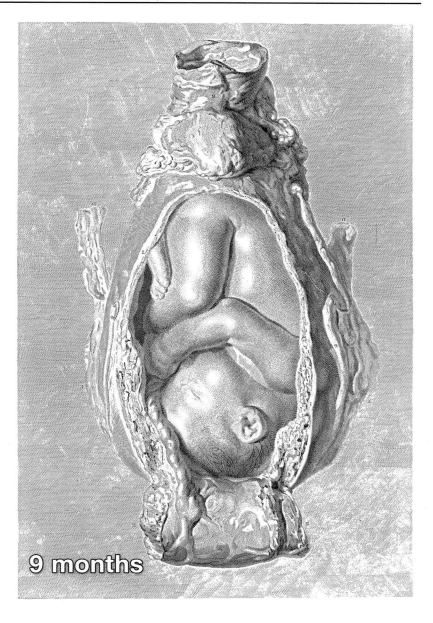

FIGURE 7-21
9 MONTHS
HUNTER 1774

FIGURE 7-22: 3D ULTRASOUND AT 38 WEEKS, SUCKING THE THUMB

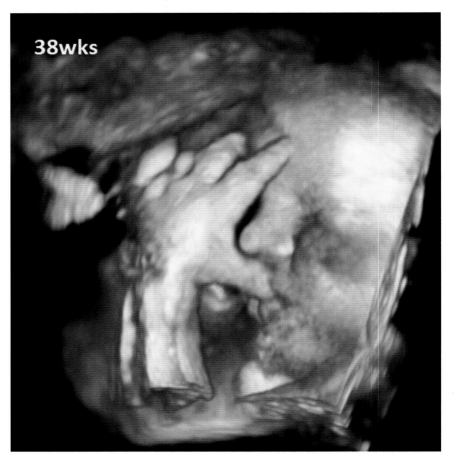

38 WEEKS — SUCKING THUMB

FIGURE 7-23: 3D ULTRASOUNDS
AT 11, 19, 27, AND 37 WEEKS
THE *IN UTERO* CONNECTIONS OF HUMAN LIFE

11 Weeks   **19 Weeks**

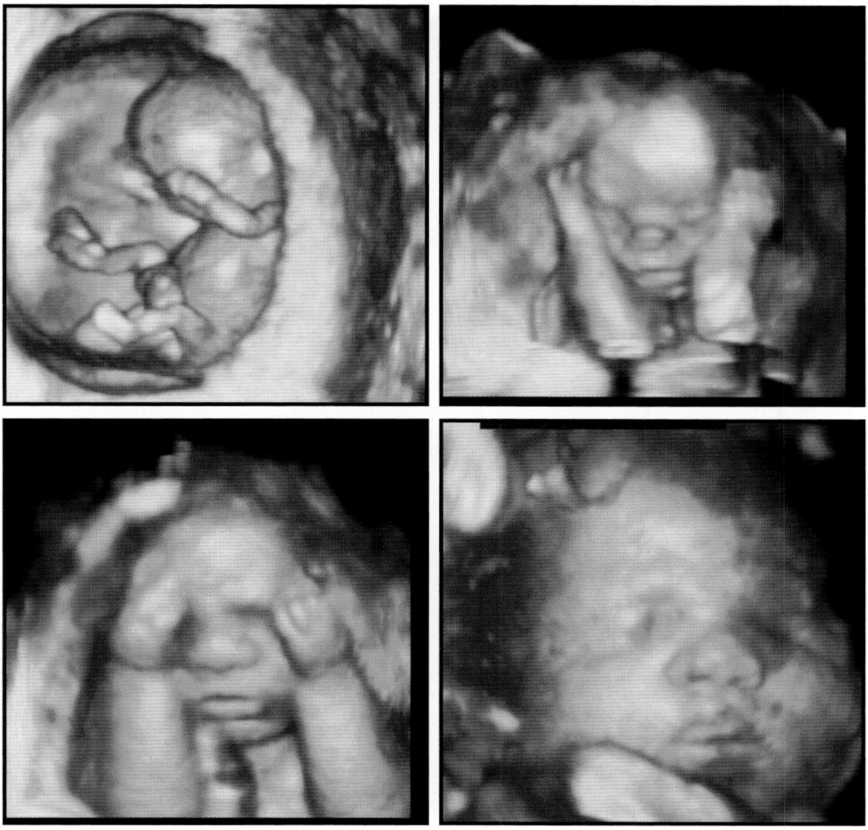

27 Weeks   **37 Weeks**

THE HUMAN LIFE CONNECTIONS: THE GROWTH AND LIFELONG MATURATION OF THE HUMAN PERSON FROM THE BEGINNING TO THE END

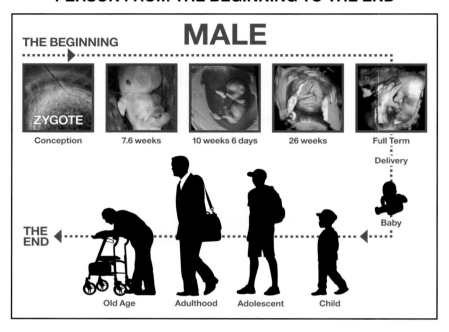

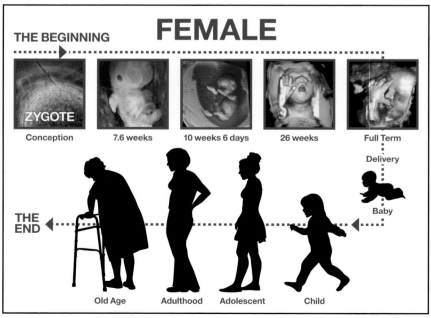

A Quiz!

Name the photograph in each of the following four photos of embryo/ fetus pictures.

See if you can match up to
a group of 5 year olds.

(For answers, look at page 171)

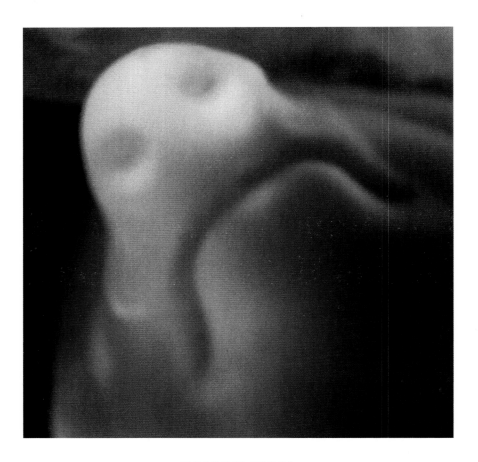

WHAT IS THIS?

1.

**THESE NEXT PHOTOS SHOW COMPARATIVE
EMBRYOLOGICAL ANATOMY**

* Pictures 1, 2, 3A, B and C From: Miller K.: What Does it Mean to be One of Us. LIFE Magazine, November 1996.
** Picture 4 from personal communication: regarding early intrauterine life with a placenta and the elephant.

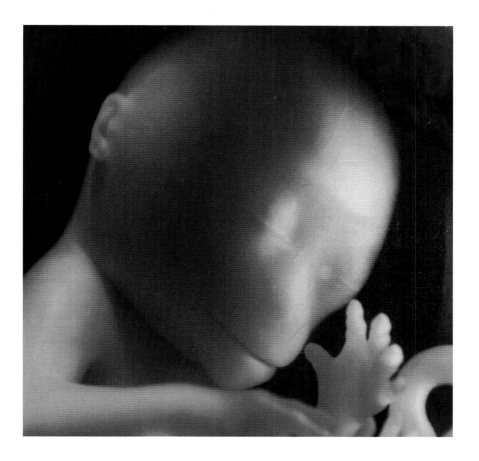

WHAT IS THIS?

2.

*The bluish discoloration over the left eye was in the original photo

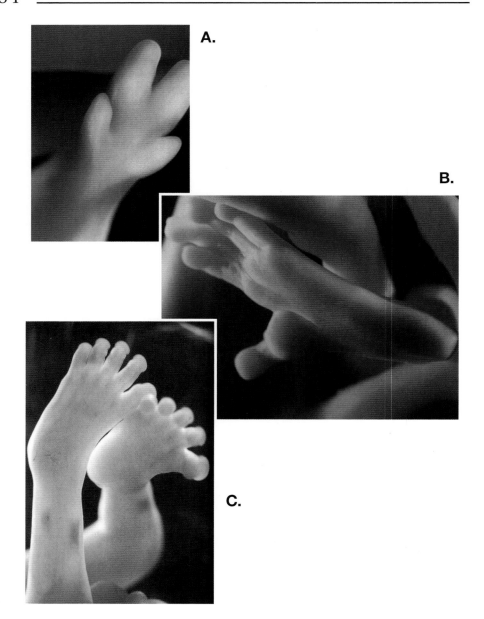

A.

B.

C.

**WHAT ARE THESE
AND FROM WHOM?**

3.

MAN'S HAND

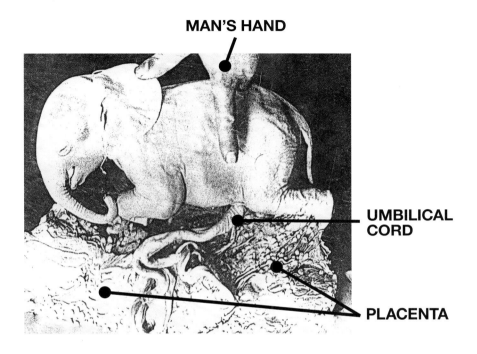

UMBILICAL
CORD

PLACENTA

WHAT IS THIS?
(USE THE MAN'S HAND TO ESTIMATE SIZE)

4.

Chapter 8

Who were Dr. Bernard Nathanson, Lawrence Lader, and Cyril Means, Jr.?

In the mid-1960s, after Lawrence Lader published his book, *Abortion*,[1] a move was begun to establish the National Association for the Repeal of Abortion Laws (NARAL) — also known as the National Abortion Rights Action League. This move was initiated by Lawrence Lader, a free-lance journalist and Dr. Bernard Nathanson, an obstetrician-gynecologist who at one time presided over the largest abortion clinic in New York City. Not too long thereafter, a law professor from New York University Law School — Professor Cyril Means, Jr., also became involved and became an attorney for NARAL. All three of these individuals were — at the time — very pro-abortion.

It's quite likely that most people who have heard at least a little about the abortion issue would not be very familiar with any of these three individuals. So this chapter goes into some detail relative to who they were and what they contributed to the move towards legalization of abortion in the United States.

It should be noted that there are a series of books that were written involving discussions of many of these people and events. The first one, as noted above, was written by Lawrence Lader and it was entitled *Abortion*.[1] It was published in 1966 by Beacon Press in Boston. Beacon Press books were published under the auspices of the Unitarian Universalist Association which generally represents a very leftist philosophy of life. The second was a series of three books written by Dr. Bernard Nathanson; the first was entitled, *Aborting America*[2] which was published in 1979. The second was entitled *The Abortion Papers*[3], and the third, *The Hand of God*[4], Regnery Publishing, Washington, DC, 2013. The fifth book was entitled *Abuse of Discretion*[5] written by Clark D. Forsythe, an attorney who worked at Americans United for Life. It was written as an inside story of *Roe v. Wade* and it revealed "new revelations from the Justices' papers"[5] and was published in 2013. *Subverted* was the most recent, published in 2015 and was written by Sue Ellen Browder[6]. The subtitle of this book was, *"How I Helped the Sexual Revolution Hijack the Women's Movement."* These six books came together to form a historical synopsis of what these various individuals meant to the pro-abortion movement and also included the approach provided by Cyril Means, Jr.

For the most part, people in the abortion-related movement — including the pro-life movement — were not familiar with many of these people and their impact. For example, *Lawrence Lader* was a free-lance journalist who, in effect, pawned himself off as an expert in medicine, law and philosophy and ***was cited no less than eight times by Blackmun as a primary reference in Roe v. Wade.*** *Cyril Means, Jr.* was a law professor who became a member of the Board of Directors of the National Association for the Repeal of Abortion laws (NARAL), and eventually was one of the association's attorneys. While he, too, was no major source of knowledge on abortion, he had a strong bias in favor of it. ***He was cited as an expert no less than seven times by Blackmun in Roe v. Wade.*** Between Lader and Means, they were cited as experts no less than 15 times in *Roe v. Wade*, **more than any other individual citations.**

Dr. Bernard Nathanson was an obstetrician-gynecologist who was the director of the largest abortion clinic in the world in New York

City and had presided over 60,000 abortions. His story is somewhat different in that he began rethinking this issue and eventually went against what he had been working so hard for. He became a defender of the unborn and an antagonist to the legalization of abortion. He eventually converted to Catholicism before his death and was a pro-life advocate. *Clark D. Forsythe* is an attorney and is Senior Council at Americans United for Life. *Sue Ellen Browder* was a writer for *Cosmopolitan* magazine at the beginning of that magazine where they basically made up stories about young women having sexual affairs with men — usually many men — and in this book, she writes about a variety of different occurrences as a writer for *Cosmo* and how Helen Gurley Brown felt that young women could be free only if they worked and did not have children. Together these sources provided extensive historical input on Lawrence Lader, Cyril Means, Jr., and Dr. Bernard Nathanson.

Starting with *Dr. Bernard Nathanson*, who got to be friends with Lawrence Lader because the two of them along with Cyril Means were all from New York City. Lawrence Lader and Bernard Nathanson were two of the co-founders of NARAL and Lawrence Lader later became the President of NARAL while Dr. Bernard Nathanson was an activist physician within the structure of NARAL. They had access to the major news release sources in New York City and put together a strategic plan which would move the political repeal of abortion laws into high gear while gaining the public's sentiment. In addition, *they peddled false statistics* — for example, the number of women who died from illegal abortion or the numbers of illegal abortions were simply made up and this was testified to, especially by Dr. Nathanson.[2,3]

It seems almost criminal that the Supreme Court of the United States would take individuals like Lawrence Lader and Cyril Means as primary resources for documentation of the various components of *Roe v. Wade*. It would almost be like taking a pre-medical student as a major source for the Court's medical justification for abortion. The Catholic Church became the main target of NARAL and was the "fall guy" that everybody could "hate." But NARAL was viewed as a "progressively" liberal organization which was moving the social structure of the United States in a direction that, of course, we all knew we needed to go (in their view).

Dr. Bernard N. Nathanson and Lawrence Lader

Dr. Nathanson and Lawrence Lader met at a dinner party in 1967 in New York. Nathanson writes:[4] "At dinner, I was seated next to a cadaverous-appearing man with a rasping voice. He introduced himself as Lawrence Lader. After some small talk, he casually mentioned that he had just published a book on abortion, a book in which he had analyzed the prevailing laws restricting abortion in the United States, ripped apart all the arguments for retaining those laws, and demanded that all such laws be struck down as medically unsound and legally unconstitutional. What he was advocating was nothing less than free access to abortion for all pregnant women, the procedure to be priced so low as to be within the means of the poorest.

"We began to talk, and the conversation lasted 8 years; in that span of time, every abortion law in the United States was struck down. The lines between pro- and anti-abortionists were drawn and the battle joined. The casualty list of that war at this writing is so long that it would take 600 Vietnam memorial walls to list all who have perished.

"Lader was a fascinating farrago of paradox, he was economically secure, having been left a considerable trust fund upon the death of his father many years before. Yet, he had worked for Vito Marcantonio, the only card-carrying Communist ever to be elected to the U.S. House of Representatives. He was an ardent feminist and a great admirer of Margaret Sanger, and a patriarchal bully in his own household. He and his wife Joan Cheery Scott, who had all but given up a promising career in grand opera for him, lived in a splendid apartment on lower Fifth Avenue in Greenwich Village; but the furnishings of the place were startlingly ascetic and of a shabby gentility. He was Jewish, but in all the years I knew him he never discussed his Jewishness. He was an erudite man of exceedingly refined taste but was maddeningly pedantic and precious in his dealings with friends and allies — and **he was obsessed with abortion** (emphasis applied).

"Partly because we lived near each other, Larry and I soon were spending a great deal of time in each other's company. He was a magazine writer with no fixed hours of work, so he would accommodate graciously my very busy schedule of practicing gynecology; teaching at Cornell Medical School; reading, writing about and teaching Joyce; all the while trying to balance domestic life against these various duties and pursuits. Our subject was invariably abortion, if not directly, then indirectly; with the election of the allegedly conservative Richard Nixon in 1968, we counted ourselves set back temporarily, but certainly not discouraged or defeated. When Martin Luther King and Robert Kennedy were assassinated in the same year, we discussed these monumental events primarily as whether they were good or bad for the abortion revolution that we were by this time scheming. Even Denny McLain's heroic 30-game winning season (a feat no major league pitcher had brought off in 35 years) had to be analyzed through the abortion prism (on balance, McLain's feat was bad as it distracted the public from serious issues such as the sexual revolution.)

"In short, I found, to my surprise, that I had been subtly dragooned into planning political strategy with Lader. By 1969, we were setting the agenda for a meeting of the leading national pro-abortion figures to take place in Chicago. Out of that meeting would emerge the fledgling National Association for Repeal of Abortion Laws (NARAL), later changed to the National Abortion Rights Action League, and currently styling itself as the National Abortion Reproductive Rights Action League. We were putting out feelers to Betty Friedan and her corps of feminists to join us in the revolution, coalition building with the Woodstock nation and crushing the dinosaurs in the movement who would settle for watered-down measures such as the ALI (American Law Institute) model penal code. Lader, I, and a handful of others such as Howard Moody, then Pastor of the Judson Memorial Church in Manhattan's Greenwich Village, with the radicals, the Bolsheviks. We would settle for nothing less than striking all existing abortion statutes and introducing abortion on demand in their place.

"Our first target of opportunity was the New York State statute prohibiting abortion unless the pregnancy threatened the life of the pregnant woman. The manipulation of the media was crucial, but easy with clever public relations, especially steady drumfire press releases disclosing the dubious results of surveys and poles that were in effect self-fulfilling prophecies, proclaiming that the American people already did believe; what all reasonable folk knew that abortion laws had to be liberalized. In the late 60s and early 70s, the media trenches were peopled with young, cynical, politically case-hardened, well-educated radicals who were only too anxious to upset the status quo, roil the waters, and rattle the cages of authority.

" … A tsunami of anti-authoritarianism washed across the land, carrying with it the drug culture, the sexual revolution, the pernicious infiltration of pornography, violent crime and a contemptuous denigration of religion. Certainties as unquestioned as the U.S. Constitution itself trembled.

"Lader sniffed the winds of change. He knew, standing in the wreckage of the 60s and watching the pillars of certainty cracking and crumbling around him, that his time had come around, that it was the perfect historical moment in which to strike again senescent rheumy-eyed authority.

"He also sensed that authority had to have a familiar form, a discernable shape, a clear and preferably noxious identity, and if at all possible, a shamefully malevolent past to point to. What better than *the Roman Catholic Church*? It was spawned in blood; it had exiled, tortured, broken and murdered millions of heretics and their followers. The Church was then actively supporting the Vietnam War, opposing the sexual revolution, denouncing the drug culture and dragging its feet on the Civil Rights Movement. *No more perfect straw man could ever have been devised.*

"So we set to work, and it was like shooting fish in a barrel. *At the start, the Flat Earth Society would have seemed to constitute a greater threat to the Roman Catholic Church in 1969 than NARAL did, we attacked at every opportunity* (emphasis applied). Our favorite tack was to blame the Church for the death of every woman from a botched abortion. There were perhaps 300 or so deaths from criminal abortions annually in the United States in the 60s[8], but NARAL in its press releases claimed to have data that supported the figure of 5,000. Fortunately, the respected biostatistician, Dr. Christopher Tietze, was our ally. Though he never actually staked himself to a specific number, he never denied the authenticity of these claims.

"… One of Lader's greatest assets in the lightening campaign was also the most striking of the paradoxes in his personality. Though posing as a champion of the poor and powerless, *he led a life of conspicuous affluence.* Playing champion of the little people, paradigmatic populace, *he nursed a fine disdain for the common man.* He often quoted the passage from Machiavelli that appeared to be his homing star:

'The people resemble a wild beast which, naturally fierce and accustomed to living in the woods, has been brought up — as it were — in a prison and in servitude and having by accident got its liberty, not being accustomed to search for its food and not knowing where to conceal itself, becomes a prey of the first who seeks to incarcerate it again.'

"It was, I think, this remorseless contempt for the egalitarian principles to which he paid such meticulous lip service that made it easy for him to understand the Rockefellers and the other principalities and powers with whom he had to deal and which made him so much more appealing and acceptable to the princes of this world than any genuine proletarian, or even any genuine sympathizer with the proletariat could have been.[7]

Lawrence Lader

Sue Ellen Browder was one of the original journalists at *Cosmopolitan* magazine and in her book, *Subverted*, she admitted that for the first 10 years of the existence of *Cosmo*, the stories that were printed at the behest of Helen Gurley Brown were all in effect *made up*. Perhaps this actually was the beginning of fake journalism, which, in turn, led ultimately to fake and deceptive science. She writes:[9]

"At *Cosmo*, in my arrogance, I thought I was capable of discernment. I was lying in print by making up anecdotes about 'civilians,' that much was true, but even so, I genuinely believed I could tell the difference between the truth that would set me free and the deceptions that would keep me in bondage. Other women, in the small-town, narrow-mindedness, might not know the truth of things as they really are. But I did. Or so I thought. But in fact, I had already been taken in as much or more by the world's deceptions as anyone around me. Unfortunately, the free press is only as free as the minds of those journalists, editors and writers who work in the field. I had already become that strange paradox of mankind that's especially commonplace among journalism: I had become both the deceiver and the deceived.

"How did this paradox come about? Well for one thing, I wasn't as smart and self-aware as I thought I was, or I would've been puking on the subway. But for another, there were many propaganda spinners in New York far more sophisticated than I. One of the subtlest of them all was *Lawrence Lader*, a Harvard grad, heir of old money, and a close friend of Betty Friedan.

"I never met Larry. Until my fifth decade of life, I hadn't even heard his name. Yet my willingness to be seduced by his secret schemes and cleverly crafted 'special plea' would lead me to embrace, defend, and market a false path to freedom that was not just reprehensible but evil. What happened behind closed doors between Larry Lader and Betty Friedan would misguide my thinking in such a way that it would change my whole life and the lives of millions of other Americans.

Browder goes on to say that,[10] "Larry met Betty Friedan in 1942 through mutual friends from Vassar. The two magazine writers, both atheists with old-left leanings, continued to see each other frequently during the 1950s in the New York Public Library's Frederick Louis Allen Writers' Room. An inner sanctum of literary camaraderie, the marble-and-wood-paneled Allen Room provided working space for eleven resident writers. The only requirement for receiving a coveted key to the tall dark-wood double doors was a contract from a book publisher. In this secluded literary hideaway, Betty wrote much of *The Feminine Mystique* and Larry started his first book, a biography of Planned Parenthood founder Margaret Sanger. During three years of interviews, as Sanger poured out her most intimate thoughts to Lader, she would become, in his words, 'the greatest influence' in his life.

"It was while working on Sanger's biography in the Allen Room that Lader first became *obsessed with abortion* as the royal road to sexual freedom. Lader scorned pregnancy as 'the ultimate punishment of sex' and idolized abortion as the ultimate way for a man and woman to enjoy 'the pleasure of sex for its own sake' without having children. The idea of death before birth — for that is what abortion is — fascinated him.

"Lader and Friedan shared many ideas in common. For example, both would one day sign the Humanist Manifesto II, an idealogical statement written in 1973 for the American Humanist Association (AHA). The model of the AHA is 'good without a God.'

"If I had read the Humanist Manifesto in my 20s, since I considered myself an 'educated and sophisticated person,' I probably would have signed it to. In many of its tenets, the Manifesto differed little from our *Cosmo* philosophy. Both shared the same core belief: That human beings are entirely in charge of the universe and each isolated individual, operating independently, must make up his or her own private rules. In many ways, humanism as it was laid out in the Humanist Manifesto II was just our *Cosmo* philosophy dressed up in a tweed jacket with a college diploma.

"Much of the Manifesto sounded quite noble. It urged the 'recognition of the common humanity of all people' and stated, 'We must learn to live openly together or we shall perish together.' Yet it also alluded to traditional religions as 'obstacles to human progress,' stated that morals 'derive their sources from human experience' and 'need no theological or ideological sanction,' and called for the 'rights' to abortion, birth control, euthanasia and suicide.

"Hidden within the Humanist Manifesto II also lay an unspoken assumption about an individual's *personhood*. The document reflected the fashionable belief that the human person is a non-worshiping being, abandoned in a vast universe to wanderlust, lonely and afraid with neither the ability nor the need to relate to an all-loving God. Explicitly denying man's deep longings for a relationship with a God Who is Love, the Manifesto claimed that traditional religions 'separate rather than unite peoples' and 'cannot cope with existing world realities.'

"Denying the existence of the 'prayer-hearing God, assumed the love and care for persons, to hear and understand their prayers and to be able to do something about them,' the Manifesto both Larry and Betty signed stated, 'No deity will save us; we must save ourselves.'

"Yet, even though Betty signed the Manifesto, the memory of her Jewish roots would remain with her and call to her throughout her life. In her memoir, *Life So Far*, published when she was nearly 80 years old, she wrote that, 'There's something in Jewish theology about your duty to save your life to make life better for those who come after. I felt that mission strongly. It wasn't enough just to start a movement for women's rights. You had to make it happen.'

"Lader, too, was Jewish. He was also a staunch believer in the 18th century Malthusian notion that the world's growing population would soon lead to global famine. He had worked for a brief stint as Executive Director of the Hugh Moore Fund, which poured millions of dollars into the population control movement during the 1960s. Perhaps the second greatest influence in Lader's life, Hugh Moore was a multimillionaire who had parlayed his idea of a disposable cup into the Dixie Cup Company which he then sold. Moore believed that the United States needed to fight the looming threat of Communism in third-world nations by keeping the poor from having 'too many' children. To mold public opinion and sway public policy makers to adopt his way of thinking, Moore wrote and published a fear-mongering little pamphlet entitled, *The Population Bomb*. In his pamphlet, he declared, 'Today, the population bomb threatens to create an explosion as disruptive and dangerous as the explosion of the atom and with as much influence on prospects for progress or disaster, war or peace. Moore predicted a coming 'population explosion' which, as Population Research Institute President, Steven Mosher, put it, 'would be the mother of all calamities, leading to widespread famine and crushing tax rates, the spread of communism, the scourge of war, plus every other imaginable environmental and social ill in between. In Moore's mind, too many babies (particularly among the poor) were the root cause of poverty, crime, and wars. If people weren't stopped from producing like rabbits, Moore insisted, the horrible consequence would be world-wide starvation. Lader agreed with him. 'It is now recognized,' Lader ominously warned in his biography of Moore, 'that we must reduce birthrates or await the inevitable disaster. We are on the way to *breeding ourselves to death*.' (Italics his).

"Larry's surefire solution to this terrifying Malthusian idea of impending disaster was abortion, not just for the poor, but also for any woman who wanted to call herself free. Betty's special idea, you will recall, was a creative work of her own which set a woman free. Larry's special idea was that unrestricted abortion would set a woman free. In this conviction, Lader had far more in common with *Cosmo's* Helen Brown (Hard Work and Sex Without the Kids Will Set You Free) than he did with Betty.

"Betty supported the legalization of abortion — for other women. Yet, personally, even when she was fired from her newspaper job for being pregnant, the possibility of aborting her own baby to save her job seemed never to have entered her heart.

"Ideologically, I was never for abortion," Betty wrote in the year 2000. "Motherhood is a value to me, and even today abortion is not … I believed passionately in 1967, as I do today, that women should have the right of choosing motherhood. For me the matter of choice has never been primarily the choice of abortion, but that you can choose to be a mother. That is as important as any right written into the Constitution.

"Larry said he tried to persuade her otherwise, that women needed abortion to be free. Yet for many years, Betty remained unconvinced."[9]

Who was Cyril Means, Jr.?

"Blackmun cited Larry's *Abortion* book no less than eight times and Cyril Means' history (*but no other historian*) (emphasis applied) another seven times. Means arbitrarily destroyed legal precedent, replacing it with a history of his own making. According to Villanova University Law-History Professor Joseph Dellapenna, author of a meticulously researched, 1,283-page volume entitled, *Dispelling the Myths of Abortion History:* By comparison, the petty lies we told at *Cosmo* were child's play.

"To continue the ruse, **many statistics of Lader's book — and later in NARAL's press releases — were completely made up. Knowing that if a true poll were taken, we would be soundly defeated, we simply fabricated the results of fictional polls,**" Nathanson revealed. "We announced to the media that we had taken polls and that 60% of Americans were in favor of permissive abortion. This is the tactic of the self-fulfilling lie. Few people cared to be in the minority.

"Lawrence Lader wrote the book, *Abortion* and likened the abortion movement to the civil rights movement, suggesting that women's "bondage to pregnancy was unjust and as evil as 18th-century slavery" … Under the guise of objective journalism, in collusion with eminent New York pro-abortion attorneys, Harriet Pilpel, Ephraim London and Cyril Means, Jr., later methodically laid out in his book a persuasive and powerful argument for abolishing all abortion laws.[12]

"Much of the bogus abortion history in his angry book (Lader's angry book) was invented by Cyril Chestnut Means, Jr., … . Means arbitrarily destroyed legal precedent, replacing it with a history of his own making.[14]

"Means propounded two hitherto unsuspected historical 'facts.' First, that abortion was not criminal in England or America before the 19th century; and second, that abortion was criminalized during the 19th century solely to protect the life and health of mothers and not to protect the lives or health of unborn children. Regardless of how many times these claims are repeated, however, they are not facts; they are myths."

"Because Dellapenna has so effectively laid out the intellectual case against the distorted history upon which *Roe v. Wade* was based, he has been publicly accused of being a Catholic, perhaps in the hope his work will thereby be discredited. Dellapenna assures his readers, "I am not a Catholic. I am and have been for most of my life, by choice, a Unitarian. Today, one might describe me as a lapsed Unitarian, for I find even that church too restrictive."

"The Lader/Means/Nathanson pro-abortion campaign was a propagandistic tour-de-force. Means highly imaginative history was a convoluted blend of fact and fiction so intricately interlaced only an extremely well-educated and diligent historian could pry the two apart. After Lader published Means fabricated history in his abortion book, Means managed to get his misstatements of historic fact published in a reputable, scholarly journal, the New York Law Forum."[14]

He then proceeded to present his radical revision of the history of abortion — a history that had been unquestioned for centuries — to the Supreme Court in an *Amicus Brief* to *Roe v. Wade*.[15] Justice Harry Blackmun, in turn, relied, "heavily and uncritically" on this history to write his abortion opinions (*Roe* and *Doe*).

"Cyril Means, you will recall, was the NARAL attorney who falsified abortion legal history, fabricating his own version almost entirely out of whole cloth.

"And yet, as the late Notre Dame theologian, Fr. James Burtchaell observed, it is "clear in this record that Justice Blackmun was indebted for the innards of his argument to two of the major strategists of the abortion movement Means and Lader.[16]

Cyril Means in a discussion on Abortion and Animation also stated the following as if he were an expert on embryology (NOT!):

"I believe that the question, When does human life begin? deserves a similar answer. The correct answer is:

It does not begin; it began — at least 3.5 million years ago. In other words, all life is one. It is poured into many individual containers, but it is all the same life.[17]

... "In other words, there are a living human spermatozoan and a living human ovum before the moment of fertilization and all that happens at that moment is that two squads of 23 chromosomes each perform a nimble quadrille on the genetic drill-field and rearrange themselves into a platoon of 46. *There is no more life, or human life, present after this rearrangement than it was before. Not only is there no more: What life there is, is the same as before, it is continuous* (emphasis applied).[17]

It is assumed that Means used the above military-like language for comic relief to cover his **totally ludicrous understanding of biologic realism** as he, in effect, endorsed (without foundation) the views of Glanville Williams.

CHAPTER 8
REFERENCES AND FOOTNOTES

1. Lader, L: Abortion. Beacon Press, Boston, 1966. (It should be noted that Beacon Press books were published under the auspices of the Unitarian Universalist Association).

2. Nathanson, BN: Aborting America. Doubleday and Co. Garden City, New York, 1979.

3. Nathanson, BN: The Abortion Papers: Inside the Abortion Mentality, Frederick Fell Publishers, New York, 1983.

4. Nathanson BN: The Hand of God: A Journey from Death to Life by the Abortion Doctor Who Changed His Mind. Regnery Publishing, Washington, DC, 2013.

5. Forsythe CD: Abuse of Discretion. The Inside Story of Roe v. Wade. Encounter Books, New York and London, 2013.

6. Browder, Sue Ellen: Subverted: How I Helped the Sexual Revolution Hijack the Women's Movement. Ignatius Press, San Francisco, 2015.

7. Op. cit.: Nathanson, BN: The Hand of God, pp. 88-93, 2013.

8. The number of maternal deaths from abortion (all causes) in the 10 years prior to Roe v. Wade was no greater than 225 and the year before Roe v. Wade it was 48 (From: National Center of Vital Statistics).

9. Op. cit.: Browder, SE, pp. 47-48, 2015.

10. Op. cit.: Browder, SE, pp. 48-51, 2015.

11. In this review, it appears to have been eight times.

12. Op. cit.: Browder, SE: p. 57, 2015.

13. Op. cit.: Browder, SE: p. 55, 2015.

14. Op. cit.: Browder, SE: p. 56, 2015.

15. Op. cit.: Browder, SE: p. 57, 2015.

16. Op. cit.: Browder, SE: p. 95, 2015.

17. From: Means, Jr., CC: Abortion and Animation: In: Hall, RE, Editor, Abortion in a Changing World. Vol. 2. Columbia University Press, New York and London, 1970, p. 10.

* Lest there be no mistake, Steven Mosher is an expert in population dynamics, and he is pro-life.

Chapter 9

A Catastrophically Lethal Ethic: The Big Bully in the Room!

In September 1948, *The World Medical Association* (to which the United States was a founding member) "After a lengthy discussion of war crimes based on information from the United Nations War Crimes Commission[1] adopted the *Declaration of Geneva* which said, "I will maintain the utmost respect for human life, from the time of conception; even under threat, I will not use my medical knowledge contrary to the laws of humanity."[2] This was followed in October 1949 by the *International Code of Medical Ethics* which stated, "A doctor must always bear in mind the importance of preserving human life from the time of conception until death."[3] At that time, Dr. Paul Cibrie, Chairman of the Committee which had drawn up the *International Code*, stated that the abortionists were in fact condemned in the *Declaration of Geneva*.[4] This was reaffirmed by the World Medical Association in 1970 with the *Declaration of Oslo*, "The first moral imposed upon the doctors' respect for human life as expressed in the clause of the *Declaration of Geneva*:

"I will maintain the utmost respect for human life from the time of conception…"[5]

Furthermore, on November 20, 1959, the General Assembly of the United Nations *unanimously* adopted the *Declaration of the Rights of the Child*. The Preamble to the Declaration stated that the child, by nature of its physical and mental immaturity, needs "special safeguards and care, including appropriate legal protections, before as well as after birth."[6] Governments were called upon to recognize the rights and freedoms set forth in the Declaration and described for their observance by legislative and other measures." In addition, the pro-abortion California Medical Association wrote in September 1970 that, "Human life begins at conception and is continuous, whether intra or extra-uterine until death."[7] Dr. Alan Guttmacher, pro-abortionist head of Planned Parenthood — World Population, wrote (in 1950) that at the exact moment of conception a new baby is created, and that "At the exact moment when a new life is initiated (fertilization), a great deal is determined which is forever irrevocable — its sex, coloring, body build, blood group, and in large measure its mental capacity or emotional stability."[8]

It is obvious that the ethical consensus existed! It seems equally obvious that the Court chose to ignore the consensus. No less than six times Justice Blackmun referred to this life as "potential" human life and on at least two occasions, he referred to the conception of a new human as "one theory of life." There is nothing theoretical about the beginning of human life and the unborn is actual not potential. The child does exist in spite of the Court's medical ignorance and prejudice, and the decision of the Court did nothing to disprove that. What it did do, of course, was to perpetrate the ignorance which is so common today in this area.

"Individual human life **begins** at conception (the union of the mother's egg with the father's sperm) (See Chapter 6) and is a progressive, ongoing continuum until **natural death** (unless, of course, an unnatural death interrupts this chain of life). This is a fact so well established that no intellectually honest physician in full command of modern medical knowledge would dare to deny it. There is no authority in medicine or biology who can be cited to refute this concept. It is not a 'theory,' as Justice Blackmun wished to so easily pass it off."[9]

The Hippocratic Oath: Although the oath is not mentioned in

any of the principle briefs submitted to the Court, Justice Blackmun thought that the discussion and devaluation of the oath, which for centuries stood as a bulwark against abortion, was necessary. He felt that it was so necessary that he apparently did independent research to make his point.[10] Why? What was there about the Hippocratic Oath that made its demise an almost absolute imperative for Justice Blackmun — such that he would independently exert judicial energy to research in order to belittle and destroy? What are the psychological imperatives that would compel those who would destroy human life to make their position ethical? [11,12,13]

"Justice Blackmun brushed aside over 2,000 years of medical history to accept a working hypothesis of one deceased historian as gospel. His entire research as evidenced in his opinion relies on the theory put forth by L. Edelstein which concludes that the Hippocratic Oath was merely the dogma of a small sect, a 'Pythagorean Manifesto' and not the expression of an absolute standard of medical conduct.[10] Edelstein reached this conclusion without the benefit of the War Crimes Commission reports following World War II.

What then? Apparently those thousands upon thousands who have taken this oath, "I will give no deadly medicine to anyone if asked, nor suggest any such counsel; and in like manner I will not give to a woman a pessary to produce abortion"[11] were only the tools (or fools) of the Pythagoreans. Do we assume, then, that with the Court's pronouncement they are henceforth released from the oath? Could not the Court have just as easily chosen the position of other scholars who have said:[12]

> But the most fascinating recent comment on the Hippocratic Oath is one which originated with *Margaret Mead*, the great anthropologist. Her major insight was that the Hippocratic Oath marked one of the turning points in the history of man. She says, "For the first time in our tradition, there was a complete separation between killing and curing. Throughout the primitive world, the doctor and the sorcerer tend to be the same person. He with power to kill had power to cure, including especially the undoing of his own killing

activities. He who had power to cure would necessarily also be able to kill."

"With the Greeks," says Margaret Mead, "the distinction was made clear. One profession, the followers of Asclepius, were to be dedicated completely to life under all circumstances, regardless of rank, age, or intellect — the life of a slave, the life of the Emperor, the life of a foreign man, the life of a defective child." Dr. Mead emphasized the fact that, "This is a priceless possession which we cannot afford to tarnish, but society always is tempting to make the physician into a killer — to kill the defective child at birth, to leave the sleeping pills beside the bed of the cancer patient," and she is convinced that, "It is the duty of society to protect the physician from such requests."

Blackmun's reflections set us back to before the Middle Ages — to pre-medieval times resisting biological realism. The medical profession has resisted this in spite of the evidence. It is sort of like, "Don't confuse me with the facts. I am happiest as a human life denier!"

For me, I have seen this evidence day in and day out and it is within the realm of all physicians and specialists in reproductive medicine to see this as well! We're living in a medical world that strives to have medical strategies that are evidence based. *Changing the meaning of words or using rhetorical ploys is not evidence — it is political strategy!* We must come out of the world of pre-medieval resistance and come into the world of biological and scientific reality! Furthermore, Blackmun truly rejected the ethical statements released by major international associations following their study of what happened in Nazi Germany and was strongly reflected in the post-war Nuremberg Trials. ***Perhaps even worse, nearly all medical schools in the United States have eliminated any declaration at their graduation ceremonies where the respect for human life has previously been upheld. This started with Roe v. Wade and has continued and expanded ever since.***

PERSONHOOD

It is said that personhood exists when there is established an inter-relationship between two human beings.[14] In fact, from the very moment of conception, this new developing human being does inter-relate with its mother and through the mother to the father. As an obstetrician with over 40 years of experience, the breast tenderness that exists almost from the moment of conception is one of the earliest signs of interaction between mother and baby. The mother knows this to be a sign of pregnancy. The early fatigue of pregnancy can in some women be significant. We have home pregnancy tests that now can diagnose pregnancy as early as eight days after conception, and a recent study has shown that a blood test for pregnancy can be observed as positive within four days of ovulation.[15] As the baby begins to grow, it puts pressure on the mother's bladder and she has to urinate more frequently. An ultrasound now can show the mother and the father the baby's heartbeat as early as 24–27 days after conception.[16]

Many of these signs and symptoms are, to all other observers, silent! But they are not silent to the mother! This interrelationship tells her that she is pregnant. It tells her that she is "with child." Eventually she will tell people, "I am having a baby." But, over all these years, the culture has tried to dehumanize the personhood that is present in the early developmental stages of human development. And yet, to state this denies the interaction that the early human embryo has with its mother. Personhood is indeed there from the moment of conception just as it is the very beginning of one's existence. The Supreme Court can view corporations and rivers and others as "persons," but they have blinders on when they cannot see the personhood of the human being in the earliest days of its development.

The Posterity Clause in the United States Constitution

Blackmun emphasizes that the term "person" in the United States Constitution is seen in several locations, but "none indicates, with any assurance" that it has any possible "pre-natal application." And yet, the very Preamble to the United States Constitution includes all future generations. The Preamble states:

> "**We the People** of the United States, in Order to form a more perfect Union, establish Justice, insure domestic Tranquility, provide for the common Defense, promote the general Welfare, and secure the Blessings of Liberty to ourselves and **our Posterity** (emphasis applied), do ordain and establish this Constitution of the United States."[17]

The word "People" means "a body of persons living in the same country under one government." The word "Posterity" means "future generations."[18]

Justice Blackmun and the Court had the opportunity to make a strong statement in defense of life given all of the advanced information and scientific enlightenment that had become available since 1774. He had the opportunity to recognize that the Constitution of the United States was set up not just for ourselves, but for all future generations (our "posterity") and that, in fact, the child in the mother's womb from the moment of conception is the beginning of each of those future generations. In fact, it is an actual generation, not just a possible generation or a potential generation. It is a generation with great potential! It is a generation that will come for all future centuries for which the Constitution stands, but it is also here now! This ultimately is why it is so important to solve the issue of when life begins. But Blackmun chose not to do this. His choice was a direct negation of the protections of the United States Constitution for existing generations and, until corrected, all future generations are at the risk of this **catastrophically lethal ethic**.

Why is it that anyone is pro-abortion? Why is it that anyone would like to take the life of an unborn child who is so helpless, so small, the most innocent of all humans, and so otherwise secure in its mother's womb? But today, it is located at **the most dangerous intersection of life!** Abortion is often portrayed as a special form of freedom, but it is really **the most lethal place** of all! It is a place that we have all been given the opportunity to survive, but we are given this opportunity while being prejudicially ignorant of what has been lost! Survival in today's world is truly the most significant of life's struggles. It is the most significant human rights issue of our day, but we must win this struggle, for the right of our unborn brothers and sisters to be born is truly at stake!

Blackmun defied and defiled modern science, ignored the progress that had been made in embryology, fetology and our understanding of the growth and development of the human person; and, as a result of the Court's decision, millions upon millions have been destroyed viciously and violently. **It needs to be stopped!**

Catastrophically Lethal: The Big Bully in the Room.

Since Roe V. Wade, many countries throughout the world have followed the Roe v. Wade lead and legalized abortion. **On the surface**, it would appear to be a simple and aesthetic solution to otherwise complex problems. But in reality, it is **vicious** and **violent**, usually a dismemberment of a new human baby. **A form of bullying that goes way beyond any of the bullying that we usually think about!** We have come to expect and accept that the medical profession will carry out these executions!

Our schools and institutions have abandoned the Hippocratic Oath and the Declaration of Geneva and replaced it with a policy of **lethalism**. One could argue that this is a direct result of the Court's acceptance and promotion of archaic scientific reasoning that, at best, would be considered pre-medieval and clearly out of touch with scientific reality. Other fallout includes the expansion into fetal experimentation, human cloning, embryonic stem cell research and most recently infanticide. Even physician-assisted suicide programs have grown. The **respect for life ethic** has slowly been removed as the Supreme Court has so strongly supported the **"death becomes a way of life" ethic.** Especially interesting is the lack of support for positive, life-supporting solutions to these issues.

A number of years ago, the Governor of the State of New York publicly stated that if you are "pro-life" then you shouldn't move to the state of New York. In January, 2019, Governor Andrew Cuomo answered that abortion in New York can now be obtained up to the time of full term and that it can be performed by non-physicians. After it was passed, the New York Legislature burst out in celebratory applause and cheering. The pinnacle of the new World Trade Center was specially lit up in pink to join the celebration. Subsequent to this, another East Coast Governor called for **infanticide,** and a U.S. Senator has made the claim that **"being pro-life"** is the same as being **"a racist."** Those who favor **abortion** are properly called **lethalists,** and it is **catastrophic**. It is **ugly, vicious,** and **violent! How out of touch can they get?**

CHAPTER 9
REFERENCES AND FOOTNOTES

1. World Medical Association Bulletin, Vol. 1, p. 22, April 1949.

2. Ibid.

3. World Medical Association Bulletin, Vol. 2, pp. 5-34, January 1950.

4. Ibid.

5. Ibid.

6. *Everyman's United Nations,* A complete handbook of the activities and evolutions of the United Nations during its first 20 years 1945-1965, Eighth Edition. United Nations, New York, p. 360.

7. "A New Ethic for Medicine and Society," California Medicine, Official Journal of the California Medical Association, 113:67-68, September 1970.

8. Guttmacher, AF: Having a Baby. Signet Books, New York, New American Library, 1950, p. 15.

9. From: Hilgers TW, Horan DJ. Abortion and Social Justice. Sheed and Ward, New York, 1972, pp. 310-311.

10. Op. cit. *Roe v. Wade,* 1973, p. 16.

11. Op. cit. Hilgers and Horan, 1972.

12. Ibid.

13. Levine Maurice: "Psychiatry and Ethics". New York: Braziller, 1972, Part II, Chapter 6, "Hippocratic Oath for Physicians."

14. Callahan D. Abortion: Law, Choice, and Morality. Macmillan, New York, NY, 1972, pp. 497–498.

15. Cole LA, Ladner DG, Byrn FW: The Normal Variabilities of the menstrual cycle. Fertil Steril 91: 522–527, 2009.

16. Saint Paul VI Institute Research. Division of Reproductive Ultrasound (2018).

17. United States Constitution. http://www.archives.gov/exhibits/charters/constitution_transcript.html.

18. Webster's II New College Dictionary. Houghton Mifflin Co., Boston, 2001, p. 814.

Chapter 10

Viability, Polarization, and Other Important Issues

The Issue of Viability

Blackmun writes in *Roe* that, "With respect to the State's important and legitimate interests in potential life, the 'compelling point' is that of *viability* (emphasis applied). This is so because the fetus then presumably has the capability of *meaningful life* (emphasis applied) outside the mother's womb. State regulation protective of fetal life after viability thus has both some logical and biological justification. If the State is interested in protecting fetal life after viability, it may go so far as to proscribe abortion during that period except when it is necessary to preserve the life or health of the mother."[1]

Traditionally, viability has meant (from a medical point of view) the ability of the baby to live *outside* the mother's womb. While medicine is often very good at selecting the proper words to describe or name things, in this case, whoever selected the term 'viability' created a problem that lacks specificity. In reality, the term viability comes from the term "viable" which means "capable of living." By itself, it doesn't have anything to do with whether that life is living inside the womb or outside the womb. In order to distinguish between the two, those interested in these subjects medically chose the term "viability" as the term which distinguishes between the capability of the fetus to live *outside* the womb (noted as being viable) and its life that exists *inside* the womb (which by subtraction means *nonviable).* So, ultimately, it's somewhat of an artificial cutoff, although Blackmun likes to point out that it is related to the "capability of meaningful life outside the mother's womb." And yet, when one introduces the term *"meaningful life"* as Blackmun did, one gets into an expanded problem that lacks definitional specificity because these are the types of terms that were used during the Third Reich. For example, who determines whether that life is "meaningful" and what are the criteria upon which these decisions become representative of a truth and are significant. In fact, *Roe* describes that viability is reached at 28 weeks and in some areas may be as early as 24 weeks. But in reality, it identifies a "moving target" which in some places in the United States today is now down to 22 weeks.

What we actually have in these situations is something we can refer to as **extracorporeal** (outside of the woman's body) **viability** and **intracorporeal** (inside the woman's body) **viability**. Whether the fetus, embryo or zygote is inside the mother's body or outside the mother's body is in reality irrelevant because in all cases, life is present — and if that life is significant later in life, let us say after birth, it is certainly of significance before that time all the way back to the moment of conception. The problem with making these designations, which are somewhat arbitrary and certainly artificial, is that the life of this human being is present in both situations and is in fact meaningful in both situations as well. So whether the fetus exists outside the mother's body or within it is ultimately not of major significance because life — the same life — exists whether it's inside the body or outside the body.

An interesting corollary to all of this, at this time, would be a procedure called *in vitro* fertilization or "test tube babies." The conception — the union of the sperm and the egg — is conducted in a petri dish outside of the woman's body, and it is very much alive. That is then transplanted into the uterus of the woman where the pregnancy continues forward if all goes well. But the embryo loss rate is quite high in this condition, mostly because it cannot yet be as successful as natural conception, implantation and subsequent growth and development. The natural peri-implantation loss in pregnancy has generally been exaggerated by IVF enthusiasts and even in the medical literature, **but when one studies it closely, one finds that the ultimate early loss of embryos is significantly below 3 percent.** This research was published in the textbook, *The Medical & Surgical Practice of* **NaProTECHNOLOGY**, Chapter 58 ("Early Pregnancy Loss: Challenging Current Paradigms"). And while a significant increase in loss of embryos prior to implantation is noted in *Roe v. Wade* and it has been an argument in favor of *in vitro* fertilization over the years, it is, in reality, not true, and it is provable. It is a fake!

One other point to be made: When a baby is born, is that baby capable of "living outside the womb?" The answer is yes it is but not independently. A newborn baby needs a lot of help from most especially his/her parents over a relatively prolonged period of time (measured in years) in order to successfully pass through these early years. They are not independent. If the baby is born prematurely at let's say 28 weeks, the baby requires expertise that the parents generally do not have so the baby can survive but only with the help of a cadre of physicians and nurses with the special training and assistance in this field of medicine. They are much more dependent than a newborn at full term and also very expensive. So where does Roe's concept of "viability" leave us for the future? Empty!

Polarization of the Body Politic

There has been a polarization in the political processes, which has produced a kind of gridlock and distrust, which only a decision like *Roe* could produce. Not only has it resulted in the vicious and violent destruction of human life, but it has not solved the problems that it was purported to solve. In fact, most of those problems have gotten worse.[2,3] In Section VIII of *Roe*, Blackmun says that, "The detriment that the State would impose upon the pregnant woman by denying this choice (whether or not to terminate her pregnancy) is apparent. Specific and direct harm … maternity, or additional offspring, may force upon the woman a distressful life and future. Psychological harm may be imminent. Mental and physical health may be taxed by childcare. There is also the distress for all concerned, associated with the unwanted child and there is the problem of bringing a child into a family already unable psychologically, and otherwise, to care for it. In other cases, as in this one, the additional difficulties and continuing stigma of unwed motherhood may be involved. All these are factors the woman and her responsible physician necessarily will consider in consultation."[4]

But, *Roe* has not solved any of the problems that it purported to solve. In fact, most of these problems have gotten worse. Since 1973, there has been a near doubling of the number of children living only with their mother. Of course, there has been an increase in the number of abortions, and the out-of-wedlock birth rate has increased from 14 to nearly 45%.[2] There has also been an increase in child abuse, violent crime, juveniles taken into police custody and an increase in teenage suicides. Furthermore, there has been a significant increase in the prematurity rate and of babies with both low birth weight and very low birth weight.[2] The Court knew this latter piece of information before it decided *Roe* and yet chose to ignore it.[5] This had happened in other countries that had legalized abortion on a widespread basis. Countless numbers of infants have been damaged as a result of this and the mental harm and distress that it has caused women (mothers) is immeasurable. Women are the ones that are struck hardest by these changes in the society. Numbers are not kept on the effect this might have on one's faith, but experience has shown that abortion is at best faith-deadening. And what does it do to our understanding of the meaning of life? When life is so devalued, its meaning is also decreased.

The Liberals, in collaboration with the radical feminist movement, have provided a group of spokespeople who are almost irrational when it comes to their cry for abortion. They try to intimidate and they ridicule, and they are ultimately extremely insensitive to the real problems of women and families. Furthermore, the Republicans have done little to better understand this issue so as to be more persuasive and of better help. The culture wonders out loud about why there is so much disunity in our politics. One needs to look no further than abortion to find the answer.

In addition, David Brooks[6] charged that, "Justice Harry Blackmun did more inadvertent damage to our democracy than any other 20th century American. When he and his Supreme Court colleagues issued the *Roe v. Wade* decision, they set off a cycle of political viciousness and counter-viciousness that has poisoned public life ever since." Regardless of what the roots of this might be, it is clear that that conflict exists and the destruction of over 60 million lives in direct violation of the *"Posterity Clause"* of the United States Constitution is bound to generate this reaction. It is not something that can be compromised. It is not something that can be talked away. It is something that desperately needs to be dealt with in a positive, constructive and protective way.

Other scholars have called for *Roe v. Wade* to be reversed.[7,8] In fact, the nation and/or the Court has before it the possibility that it can actually bring up-to-date — given current technological advances — our understanding of life before birth and the absolutely essential nature of it to the beyond-birth life of all of us. Without life before birth, there is no life beyond birth. Without life before birth, there is no discovery of insulin. Without life before birth, there is no man that reaches the moon. Without life before birth, there is no Oprah Winfrey. Life before birth is a pre-requisite for all of us.

We need to move away from the intellectually dishonest spin that led to *Roe v. Wade*. We need to come to grips with reality. When Chief Justice Warren Burger said in his assent to *Roe* that "plainly, the Court today rejects any claim that the Constitution requires abortion on demand,"[9] it may be one of the most extraordinarily naïve statements ever made by a Chief Justice of the United States Supreme Court. It is cold, insensitive and it lacks a sense of reality! Abortion on demand is what the Court ordered and abortion on demand is what we received!

Blackmun's Reputation as a Poor Writer

"To sort out the abortion mess, the first person Harry turned to for help was his old friend Tom Keys, head of the Mayo Clinic Medical Library[10] in Rochester, Minnesota. Blackmun had spent nine of the best years of his life working at Mayo as a "doctor's attorney." Tom immediately rallied his library staff and began sending Harry articles on the Hippocratic Oath and the abortion industry."[11]

Interestingly enough, this was a time when I was a resident in the Department of Obstetrics & Gynecology at the Mayo Graduate School of Medicine. After *Roe v. Wade* came out, I went to the Mayo Clinic's Library to see whether or not I could determine if any of the textbooks on embryology had been checked out by the Blackmun group. I got information from the young librarian who was working the evening shift that Blackmun had definitely been there and had spent about a week reviewing various materials. So I went into the stacks and checked every embryology textbook in the Mayo Clinic Medical Library (and that was a large number) and none of them had been checked out by Harry Blackmun or any of his associates.

"When at last in mid-May, Harry showed a draft of his *Roe* opinion for the first time to one of his politically leftist law clerks, the clerk claimed to be 'astonished' the draft was so crudely written and poorly organized. When he circulated the draft on May 18, 1972 to the other Justices they were 'disappointed.'

"Why were Douglas and Marshall so disappointed?" Browder asked. "Catholic feminist, Mary Meehan suggests one possible reason."[12] Meehan reports, "Justices Douglas and Marshall had been lacking in sexual restraint — to put it mildly — well before the 60s and the problems of both were aggravated at times by heavy drinking. Perhaps they realized that legal abortion would be extremely helpful to *men* — enabling them to escape paternity suits, years of child support, social embarrassment, and the wrath of betrayed wives. But none of this, of course, would be mentioned in the Court's opinions," Meehan reports.

"In any case, when Harry failed to produce a competent pro-abortion draft of his opinions, he got flack from his colleagues. … Having vowed to do his best to arrive at something which would command a Court," Harry withdrew the draft asking that all copies be returned to him. He planned to do more work on his opinions over the summer while Blackmun immersed himself in research at the Mayo Clinic Medical Library in July, 1972. Meanwhile, his politically liberal $15,000-a-year law clerk, George T. Frampton, Jr., age 28, volunteered to stay in Washington until early August to help research and draft the opinions. The two talked by phone almost daily.[13]

Browder wrote[14] that "an early draft Harry wrote on the history of abortion in his small, cramped long-hand reveals he was still struggling. Writing is difficult and Harry wasn't much of a writer. On the subject of abortion, Harry was finding it hard to think clearly. … Young George, on the other hand, was an excellent writer. He graduated from Harvard Law School in 1969 (where he was the Managing Editor of the Harvard Law Review), and he had at his fingertips an extraordinarily handy resource — a highly persuasive book entitled, *Abortion:*

The First Authoritative and Documented Report on the Laws and Practices Governing Abortion in the U.S. and Around the World and how — for the Sake of Women Everywhere — They Can and Must Be Reformed. Yes, indeed, it was Larry Lader's masterpiece of propaganda,[15] the same book that had so greatly impressed Betty Friedan.

"Lader's masterpiece of propaganda supplied much of the historic background Blackmun's opinion had previously lacked, but more important, Lader's book provided a coherent form or template that tied together the many disconnected fragments of thought that had previously kept Blackmun's abortion opinions from working. In the new sections of the history of abortion written by George and dated August 10, 1972, Lader's book suddenly appears in the footnotes for the first time.[16]

"In a lengthy five-page, single-spaced letter, typed on legal-sized paper, which he sent to Harry along with the draft, George made an unusual suggestion. He suggested that Harry consider *circulating his new draft before it was cite-checked by a clerk* (emphasis applied). Cite-checking is a detailed fact-checking to insure that a judicial decision is sound. Why would a junior law clerk suggest circulating a draft that hadn't been cite-checked?

"George was eager for Harry to circulate his draft before oral arguments were re-heard in October for three reasons: He wrote that circulating the revised draft before oral argument would "nail down [Blackmun's] keeping the assignment … (and) should influence questions and thinking at oral argument," and "might well influence voting." "Though George stated he would not recommend delayed cite-checking "as standard operating procedure, he thought that in this particular case, the benefits strongly outweighed the disadvantages.

"We don't know when or even if the history section in Blackmun's abortion opinions were ever cite-checked. But we do know that if it happened, the fact-checking was faulty. For when Blackmun accepted Larry Lader, a mere magazine writer, as a reliable authority on history, philosophy and theology, he became as a blind man following a blind guide. Despite his best efforts, Harry failed to see he had embraced a well-crafted verbal image mistaking it for the truth.

"Let us be very clear about what happened here. The picture that emerges from Blackmun's papers, *available for public inspection at the U.S. Library of Congress*, is that of a Justice who, in the words of Pulitzer

Prize-winning, pro-abortion historian, David J. Garrow, "ceded far too much of his judicial authority to his clerks." It is plain from the inspection of Blackmun's papers that his clerks made historically significant and perhaps decisive contributions to *Roe* and *Doe*" — a degree of involvement Garrow calls "indefensible."[16]

"Lader set himself up as an authority on centuries of abortion legal history and also on two millennia of Catholic teachings about abortion — and Blackmun and his clerk fell for the ruse. In the final version of the *Roe v. Wade* decision, Lader's masterpiece of propaganda is cited at least eight times and Cyril Chestnut Means scholarly papers are cited another seven times."

What Has Been Lost?

There have been well over 60 million abortions performed in the United States since *Roe* was ordered. This is a very conservative estimate because it does not include abortions that come from *in vitro* fertilization clinics or abortions that have been performed in a doctor's office with medicine such as RU-486. The total number may exceed even 70 or 80 million. Thus any comment about what has been lost would be unfortunate for sure.

In Table 10-1 based upon an estimate of over 30 million abortions of unborn children who would now be in the age group of 18 to 39, an estimate of the number of select occupations lost since *Roe* was ordered. Primary and secondary school teachers head the list. Registered nurses, construction workers, carpenters, physicians and surgeons and farmers all number well in excess of 100,000. Even biological and medical scientists and athletes and coaches number greater than 50,000. Others, including artists, musicians, singers, aerospace engineers, news analysts and reporters are all listed and, of course, there are many others not listed.

Could it be that we have aborted the individual who would have found a cure for AIDS, muscular dystrophy or cancer? Or could it be that we have lost other great contributors to our culture and our social well-being?

Keep in mind that Charles Best was only 22 years old when he co-discovered insulin,[17] or Akaine Kramarik who is now 23 years old is a self-taught painter[18] whose first completed self-portrait sold for $10,000 and between ages 10-12, she appeared on national television programs. Or how about Vanessa-Mae Nicholson who is now 38 years of age, but at age 10 made her debut with the London Philharmonic.[19] At age 11, she was the youngest ever student in the Royal College of Music and was described by its Director as a "true child prodigy, like Mozart and Mendelssohn." She was the youngest violin soloist to record both the Tchaikovsky and Beethoven violin concertos at age 13. Many of the world's greatest contributors have been young people. We will, of course, never know what we have lost because these lives were forever terminated from this planet.

TABLE 10-1

ESTIMATED NUMBER OF SELECTED OCCUPATIONS LOST SINCE *ROE v. WADE* (JANUARY 22, 1973) CURRENT AGES 18–39

Occupation	Estimated Number Lost since *Roe v. Wade*[1]
Primary and Secondary School Teachers	1,173,381
Registered Nurses	642,566
Construction Workers	284,964
Carpenters	251,439
Physicians and Surgeons	181,595
Farmers	139,688
Biological and Medical Scientists	53,081
Athletes, Coaches	50,288
Artists	41,906
Musicians, Singers	33,525
Aerospace Engineers	27,938
News Analysts, Reporters	16,763

1. Estimates calculated from: Section 12, Labor Force, Employment and Earnings. U.S. Census Bureau Statistical Abstract of the United States, 2011.

Some might argue that criminals and welfare-dependent individuals also might have been aborted ostensibly creating a positive for abortion. But, before one argues in this eugenic light (which itself is violent and disrespectful of human life), one needs to assess the role that abortion itself has played in creating an environment (a culture of death) for encouraging these very behaviors.

Decision is the Attending Physician's

"For the stage prior to approximately the end of the first trimester, the *abortion decision and its effectuation must be left to the medical judgement of the pregnant woman's attending physician.*

"This holding, we feel, is consistent with the relative lessons and example of medical and legal history with the lenity of the common law, and with the demands of the profound problems of the present day."[20] It is interesting that Roe v. Wade never said that the abortion decision is the woman's and hers alone! It was **not** a decision that argued for a woman's **"right to choose!"** or to **"control her own body!"** or **"reproductive freedom!"**

Right to Privacy

"The Constitution does not explicitly mention any right of privacy."[4] The last sentence of Chief Justice Warren Burger's assent says, "Plainly the court today rejects *any claim that the Constitution requires ... abortion on demand.*"[9]

Father's Rights

"Neither in this opinion nor in *Doe v. Bolton*, post, do we discuss the father's rights,"[21] if any exist in the constitutional context, in the abortion decision. No paternal right has been asserted in either of the cases and the Texas and the Georgia statutes on their face take no cognizance of the father. We are aware that some statutes recognize the father under certain circumstances ... we need not now decide whether provisions of this kind are constitutional"[22] (but the absence of any rights of the father when the child is the product of both a mother and a father seems so disjointed, artificial, and absent the important role of the father).

"IT IS SO ORDERED!"

CHAPTER 10
REFERENCES

1. Op. cit., *Roe v. Wade*, 1973, p. 48.

2. Hilgers TW: Blinders, Beaufort Books, New York, 2018.

3. Hilgers TW: Disturbing Trends in the Healthcare of Women, Children and Families. In: Hilgers TW: The Medical and Surgical Practice of **NaProTECHNOLOGY**. Pope Paul VI Institute Press, Chapter 1, Omaha, NE 2004.

4. *Roe v. Wade*, January 22, 1973, p. 36.

5. Amicus Brief of Certain Physicians, Professors, and Fellows of the ACOG in Support of Appellees. In the Supreme Court of the United States, October Term, 1971, No. 70-18, *Roe v. Wade* and 70-40 *Doe v. Bolton*.

6. Brooks, David: Roe's Birth and Death, New York Times, April 21, 2005

7. As cited in Greenhouse L, Siegel RB: Before (and after) Roe v. Wade: New Questions about Backlash. Yale Law Journal, 120:2028-2087, 2011.

8. Delahunty, RJ: Federalism and Polarization. The University of St. Thomas School of Law Legal Studies Research Paper Series. http://papers.ssrn.com/sol3/papers.cfm?abstract_id=979848.

9. Burger, Mr. Chief Justice Warren: Concurring Opinion in Roe v. Wade (70-18) and Doe v. Bolton (70-40), United States Supreme Court, January 22, 1973, p. 2.

10. Browder SE: Subverted: How I Helped the Sexual Revolution Hijack the Women's Movement. Ignatius Press, San Francisco, 2015, p. 92.

11. Time Magazine: The Decision Blow by Blow, February 5, 1973.

12. Op. cit., Browder, 2015, p. 93.

13. Op. cit., Browder, 2015, p. 94.

14. Op. cit., Browder, 2015, p. 94.

15. Lader L: Abortion. Beacon Press, Boston, 1966.

16. Op. cit., Browder, 2015.

17. Charles Herbert Best. http://bantingandbest.com/node/5, 2012.

18. Akaine Kramarik: http://en.wikipedia.org/wiki/Akiane_Kramarik, 2012.

19. Vanessa-Mae Nicholson: http://www.guinnessworldrecords.com/world-records/2000/youngest-recorded-violinist, 2012.

20. *Roe v. Wade*, January 22, 1972, p. 49.

21. *Roe v. Wade*, January 22, 1973, p. 50.

22. Ibid, Footnote 67.

Chapter 11

Summary of Investigation

This chapter, will summarize for the reader the various important scientific components that were specifically in error in *Roe v. Wade* and *Doe v. Bolton*. In order to read this for its major effect on your understanding, the item is mentioned in the left column and then on the right there is a column which is there to summarize for the reader whether it is **settled science**, **fake science** or a **deceptive** presentation:

ITEM FROM *ROE v. WADE*	SETTLED SCIENCE, FAKE OR DECEPTIVE SCIENCE
• There are **three out of three major scientific errors** in *Roe v. Wade* and *Doe v. Bolton* and it involves the three major areas of science that was cited in *Roe* and/or *Doe*. These were evaluated in Chapters 1 through 7.	
A. A frequent estimate provided to the Court by the ACOG through an *Amicus Brief* was that "over 1 million criminal abortions occurred in the United States each year resulting in an estimated 5,000 maternal deaths annually."	A. Both of these numbers were presented without scientific evidence that either was true. Dr. Nathanson confirmed that they **were "made up" (fake science)**.

B. The mortality rate from legal abortion was presented as **23.3 times** safer than the mortality from normal (ordinary) childbirth. This was declared to be **"established medical fact."**

B. The mortality rate from "normal" or "ordinary" childbirth is **zero**. If a mother dies relative to childbirth, it is not "normal" or "ordinary."

The data was presented by the Court in a way that was **deceptive** to the reader and **it was spun** so as to position itself in a clearly pro-abortion position. It was **NOT "established medical fact!"**

C. The claim that there was **"new embryological data"** that "the beginning of life is not an event," but is a "process" that goes back over 3 million years. This was presented as an alternate explanation of when life begins. This was (and is) clearly **fake science.**

C. This appears to have its origin from an article written by Glanville Williams, who at the time was the President of the Abortion Law Reform Association of England (1956).

One of the books that Blackmun cites was written by Gordon Rattray Taylor, a futuristic science journalist. Taylor emphasizes that the very real potential exists for the **"cheapening of life"** with these approaches. But this was **selected out of the analysis** presented by Blackmun.

D. Blackmun's review of the personhood of the unborn in *Roe v. Wade* was based upon the following physicians, philosophers and theologians, mostly Aristotle up to 322 B.C.; the physicians he cited were Hippocrates, Soranus of Ephesus, and Galen, 462 B.C. to 200 A.D. and two theologians, St. Augustine and St. Thomas Aquinas from 354 A.D. through 1,274 A.D.

D. **Blackmun ignored and discarded a great deal of work that was done from Leonardo Da Vinci through Davenport Hooker (1510 to 1939 A.D.).** This period of time consists of a great deal of work that could be called an **"Age of Enlightenment"** in the science regarding the growth and development of the unborn human person and pregnancy related science.

E. Blackmun stated in his review of history, "What is really pertinent here is the fact that when those trained in the respective disciplines of *medicine, philosophy* and *theology* are unable to arrive at any consensus, the judiciary *at this point in man's knowledge* (January 22, 1973) is not in a position to speculate as to the answer" (emphasis applied). He purposely left out the most important information and knowledge that is critical to our understanding: By leaving out the historical perspective *as it existed* **"at this point in man's knowledge"** (January 22, 1973).

E. Blackman's review of philosophy and theology ended at 1274 A.D. and his review of medicine (i.e. science) ended at 200 A.D. when the knowledge and understanding of prenatal life was virtually unknown to any extent. This left the historical review in *Roe* designed to **deceive** and be used to promote the pro-abortion point of view of pregnancy-related science. Blackmun's historical review was **pre-medieval** and there really is no way he was not aware of this. His perspective was designed to justify the final pro-abortion decision while trying to make the pseudo-intellectual appear to be intellectual.

F. Blackmun **attempted to re-write the facts of human biology without any scientific substance to his claim. This is perhaps one of the most egregious attempts by a major authoritative body to re-write science without any scientific validation.** Human life begins at the moment of conception — at that moment when the sperm and egg unite — and **this is a scientific fact!** It is at this moment that a totally new and unique individual, never before in existence, never again to be duplicated, comes to be. This origin of a new human life is strongly supported by the testimony of the scientific community (which was ignored in *Roe* and *Doe*) most of whom spent their lives studying early human development.

F. Citations and quotations from scientists started in this investigation with the annual meeting of the **American Medical Association** address delivered by the Chairman on the section of Medical Jurisprudence **June 10, 1887 and published in the Journal of the American Medical Association (JAMA).**

G. "The life of the foetus commences at the moment of conception ..." "but this represents only one 'Theory of Life.'"

G. Nineteen citations from scientists who have specifically studied human embryology from 1887 to 1972 asserting and supporting the fact that **human life begins with the union of the sperm and the egg commonly referred to as the "moment of conception."** *Settled science!*

H. The **single most important human cell (SMIHC)** is the **zygote**. The **zygote** is not potential human life, but **human life with potential.** But this was not recognized in *Roe* or *Doe*.

H. The **zygote** is an extraordinary cell with capabilities beyond all other cells in the human body because it is programmed to be so absolutely significant to the ongoing growth and development of the new human person. Blackmun likes to refer to this as potential human life which he does over and over and over again in *Roe*. And yet there's nothing "potential" about it. **It is actual human life! It is human life with potential.**

The human zygote is the single most important human cell (SMIHC)! It is a cell that precedes all stem cells. It is the originating cell of each individual human life. It has extraordinary capabilities. We all started with the SMIHC and, if our lives have any value now, the SMIHC surely had value then.

Many people like to say that this is a "belief." By putting it into the context of a belief, it is made to seem like one has to have a special faith to be able to see the unborn in its reality. And yet, none of that is true. **This is a scientific observation — objective, species specific, reproducible and enlightened. We have made a gross error as a nation and culture in denying it.**

After ignoring and purposely rejecting 400 years of scientific progress and our understanding of the growth and development of the human being *in utero*, Blackmun says that he was influenced by the development of "new embryological data ..." and that conception is "a process over time, rather than an event." He used seven citations to justify this. One would presume that they were all from credible scientific sources, but five of them were from law reviews and two of them were from lay science books. **None of them were credible scientific sources.** He accepted a small minority view of life (similar in context to the flat-earth society) and **actually rejected the consensus!**

The Picture Dictionary of the growing and developing human person *in utero* as shown in Chapter 7 is additionally supported by the video that is present in association with this book *(www.know-reality.us)*. This section is relatively self-explanatory and includes the videotaped sequences of the work of Davenport Hooker, PhD, at the University of Pittsburgh. Dr. Hooker used a horse hair (this is 1939 remember) and in that he was able to capture on motion picture film the response of the embryo to outside stimulation from early in pregnancy. These video sequences show definitively the ability of the embryo and fetus to respond to this type of stimulation. This is supported by the active movement of the early human life at 10 weeks 6 days (gestational age) in an undisturbed *in utero* picture by 4-dimensional, real-time ultrasound (this is 8 weeks, 6 days fetal age).

While pictures of the growth and development of the human fetus have been shown many times over the years, there are pictures that have never been seen by many people and so they are really especially extraordinary because the work of Professor Hooker is really very unique. The reader needs to emerge himself or herself in these photographs to get a real sense of what's happening here.

Dr. Bernard Nathanson was a Co-Founder of the National Association for the Repeal of Abortion Laws (NARAL) and he teamed up with Lawrence Lader, a magazine writer in establishing NARAL. Dr.

Nathanson at one point presided over the largest abortion clinic in New York City. Later he converted to Catholicism and became an antagonist to the movement on abortion. Although by this time the work that he, Lawrence Lader and Cyril Means, Jr. worked on and developed had resulted in an enormous amount of damage.

These three individuals teamed up to begin the assault on laws that protected the unborn. Lawrence Lader published a book entitled, *"Abortion"* and he came off as an expert in the philosophy and theology of abortion and the law and he was cited **eight times** in *Roe v. Wade* — **the most of any individual source.** And yet, **he was not a historian and was not a person who had any direct expertise in any of this. He was, however, obsessed by abortion.**

Lader wrote the book *"Abortion"* and likened the abortion movement to the civil rights movement, suggesting that women's "bondage to pregnancy was unjust and as evil as 18th century slavery." It was truly one of the most extraordinary statements with regard to pregnancy and womanhood that could ever have been stated.

Cyril Means, a professor of law at the New York University School of Law was also obsessed with abortion and was himself **cited seven times** in *Roe v. Wade* and yet he was not a valid authority on abortion legal history. In a 1,283-page book entitled *"Dispelling the Myths of Abortion History,"* Professor Joseph Dellapenna did an analysis of Means work and revealed that he **replaced abortion history with one of his own making** destroying legal precedent. Means was himself a biologic denier and adopted this concept. He once said that "I believe that the question, When does human life begin? deserves a similar answer. The correct answer is: it does not begin; it began — at least 3.5 million years ago. In other words, all life as one is poured into many individual containers, but it is all the same life." As I looked at the question of whether or not ethical consensus existed with regard to abortion, it is clear that there was a consensus but that it seems equally obvious that **the Court chose to ignore the consensus.**

This has led to a **bioethic which is corrupt**, it leaves the single **largest group of innocent human beings without any legal protection, and places their protection as the single largest human rights issue in our nation's history.**

Chapter 12

Conclusions

Since January 22, 1973, well over 60 million abortions have been performed in the United States, and it may be as high as 70 to 80 million. This represents a mind-boggling number of human lives that have been wiped from the face of the earth. Abortion is a violent, vicious and lethal assault on human life. This investigation makes it clear that the **United States Supreme Court,** in *Roe v. Wade* and *Doe v. Bolton*, acted with a **pro-abortion, activist and prejudicial mindset.** This is especially evident with Blackmun using Lawrence Lader as *his most cited reference*[1,2] while completely ignoring the "masterpiece" of Flanagan[3] and the extraordinary work of Davenport Hooker. The decision is noteworthy for its *lack of scholarship, extraordinary bias* and *its approach to pregnancy-related science that is literally from before the Middle Ages. It is intellectually dishonest at its core!*

It has been pointed out in this analysis that the ***human zygote is a very unique and powerful cell.*** It is a single cell that is much more powerful than a stem cell. It is the first presence of a *human zygote* that has ultimately led to all of the major discoveries and development in the history of the world; and it is the presence of *human zygotes* that allows the world to go on. It was a *human zygote*, for example, that led to the cure for polio or the discovery of penicillin. It was a *human zygote* that led to the construction of the first automobile and even the environmentally-friendly wind turbine. It was the first presence of a *human zygote* that eventually broke the world record for the fastest 100-meter run. The existence of our own *human zygote* led to our own presence on this planet.

Ultimately, this investigation has unveiled an enormous intellectual and scientific gap that stands out in Blackmun's decision. He purposely supported his own idea and theory of life which is not supported by the science of the growth and development of the unborn human person. To do this, he completely ignored and purposely rejected the most important 400 years of scientific understanding of human life *in utero*. In doing this, **the Court violated its most important dictum to be fair and impartial.**

In 1969, at my graduation from medical school, I stood with my class and recited the *Declaration of Geneva* which said: "I will maintain the utmost respect for human life, from the time of conception; even under threat, I will not use my medical knowledge contrary to the laws of humanity."[4] This Declaration was adopted by the World Medical Association (WMA) in 1948 (after a lengthy discussion of war crimes"[4] and after Edelstein's book but long before *Roe)*[5]. This was followed by the 1949 *International Code of Medical Ethics* which supported the Declaration.[6] In 1970, three years before *Roe*, the WMA reaffirmed this "respect for human life from the time of conception" in the *Declaration of Oslo.*[7] Ethical and biological consensus existed before *Roe* and Justice Blackmun tore it apart. **The Court and the nation need to own up to this grave error and remedy this injustice by bringing the unborn generation back into the world of human existence to which it rightly belongs.** To ignore this impales all human rights on a stake called **lethal relativism**. This is extraordinarily dangerous to our free society: its future and its very survivability.

The Political Distrust

There has been a polarization in the political processes, which has produced a kind of gridlock and distrust, which only a decision like

Roe could produce. Not only has it resulted in the vicious and violent destruction of human life, but it has not solved the problems that it was purported to solve. In fact, most of those problems have gotten worse. In Section VIII of *Roe*, Blackmun says that, "The detriment that the State would impose upon the pregnant woman by denying this choice (whether or not to terminate her pregnancy) is apparent. Specific and direct harm … maternity, or additional offspring, may force upon the woman a distressful life and future. Psychological harm may be imminent. Mental and physical health may be taxed by childcare. There is also the distress for all concerned, associated with the unwanted child and there is the problem of bringing a child into a family already unable psychologically, and otherwise, to care for it. In other cases, as in this one, the additional difficulties and continuing stigma of unwed motherhood may be involved. All these are factors the woman and her responsible physician necessarily will consider in consultation."[1]

But, *Roe* has not solved any of the problems that it purported to solve. In fact, most of these problems have gotten worse. Since 1973, there has been a near doubling of the number of children living only with their mother. Of course, there has been an increase in the number of abortions, and the out-of-wedlock birth rate has increased from 14 to nearly 45%. There has also been an increase in child abuse, violent crime, juveniles taken into police custody and an increase in teenage suicides. Furthermore, there has been a significant increase in the prematurity rate and of babies with both low birth weight and very low birth weight.[8,9] The Court knew this latter piece of information before it decided *Roe* and yet chose to ignore it. This happened in other countries that had legalized abortion on a widespread basis.[10] Countless numbers of infants have been damaged as a result of this and the mental harm and distress that it has caused women (mothers) is immeasurable. Women are the ones that are struck hardest by these changes in the society. And what does it do to our understanding of the meaning of life? When life is so devalued, its meaning is also trashed. And this also has a direct impact on those who are living their lives outside the womb.

Social liberals, in collaboration with the radical feminist movement, have provided a group of spokespeople who are almost irrational when it comes to their cry for abortion. They try to intimidate and they ridicule, and they are ultimately extremely insensitive to the real problems of women and families. Furthermore, the Conservatives have done little to better understand this issue so as to be more persuasive and of better help. The culture wonders out loud about why there is so much disunity in our politics. One needs to look no further than abortion to find the answer.

Settled Law? Settled Science?

In the introduction to this book, the concept that *Roe v. Wade* and *Doe v. Bolton* were "settled law" was introduced. It is, of course, not an original thought to me, but it is important in a pluralistic context so that the scientists, the law and the public as a whole will have a complete understanding of where we are. We now can answer the question of whether or not it is "settled law?" or, for that matter, "settled science?"

With regard to these two Supreme Court decisions being "settled law?" we can only hope and pray that the conscience of a nation is not willing to accept that distinction because it is far from being settled. Associate Justice Harry Blackmun along with his ghost writers put forth a legal concept which was in essence **established on fake and/or deceptive science**. Questions of science in pregnancy-related issues are sometimes thought of as being too complex. While, at its core, the prime subject has hidden itself from public view for most of the centuries and millennia that human beings have existed on this earth. But over the last 150 years (culminating a 400-year **"Age of Enlightenment"**) with a significant sense of **scientific reality** it is now known that **human life does begin at conception** (the fertilization of the egg by the sperm). This was all developed and understood for about 100 years before these Supreme Court decisions. It is for that reason that I have focused in this book on the science at the time that *Roe v. Wade* and *Doe v. Bolton* were "so ordered!" When one looks at the science that was available in 1973 and a number of areas relative to abortion and pregnancy-related science, we see that what was presented to the Court was a **science that was either fake or deceptive** (and much of it was just fake!).

The scientific questions were a big part of *Roe* and *Doe*, but **they were manipulated,** political spin if you will, to achieve a certain goal. That goal was to put everyone figuratively into an overcrowded room with only one exit and it was marked "Abortion!" It was rhetorically false but in its own way disturbingly presented and with a large dose of ridicule. This could be summarized in three principle points:

(1) There were nowhere near 5,000 to 10,000 maternal deaths due to criminal (back alley) abortion in the years leading up to *Roe* and *Doe*. This was a "scare tactic" hitting at an emotional response. **This number was falsely magnified by a factor of at least 100–200 times;**

(2) It was deceptively presented as "established medical fact" that *normal and/or ordinary childbirth* was 23.3 times more dangerous than a first-trimester abortion. **The mortality rate from normal or ordinary childbirth is zero;**

(3) The Court's view of the beginning of human life used a concept which was promoted as "new embryological data" which is **false and incorrect — completely!** In fact when human life begins was well-established by 1973, there was a scientific consensus among those who were experts in embryology. But a very small minority viewpoint similar to the concepts that the Flat Earth Society would promote were chosen to confuse people and have the reader feel like this aspect of the problem was intellectually sound.

So, the scientific principles were actually established by 1973 but were purposely kept from the public except for one small statement in *Roe v. Wade* and *Doe v. Bolton* suggesting that their existence was well known. The main principle had to do with human life beginning at conception. That intellectual concept hasn't changed for over 150 years now and there is no indication that it's going to change although we may better understand it, we may have a better perception of it. Important ultimately is that **the science was also settled,** but *Roe v. Wade* and *Doe v. Bolton* did not present to the public or to the Court the principles of that knowledge, but took a minority viewpoint as gospel. **This was done on purpose so as to make the case that abortion does not kill a human being.** It made it sound like the science supports this conclusion. But **the science that was contained in those decisions was purposely inaccurate because of a sloppy and prejudiced presentation of "the science" and a sloppy and prejudiced review presented as truth by non-scientists. Since the science is so inaccurate, how can the law be settled?** Ultimately, if the Supreme Court made such a major error in its assessment and presentation of the facts of the case and was as erroneous as it was in *Roe* and *Doe*, then **clearly the law is the one that is not settled! It is ultimately smoke and mirrors, a lie and deception so the American people could be fooled!**

It is, however, **extremely important that the law get it right!** Right now, we have a whole class of innocent human beings which are a part of the "posterity" that is referred to in the United States Constitution, that are basically deemed to be "non-existent" and without Constitutional protection! **It is so important that the Court revisit this and get it right so that all subsequent decisions can eventually be properly interpreted within the context of the truth of biologic realism and this huge inequity can once and for all be erased from our assessment and deliberation of various aspects of the law relative to the science that supports the presence of an individual who is ultimately being violently and destructively erased from life on this planet.** It is a **catastrophically lethal ethic!** The *big bullies* in the room are the grown adults, the *true victims* are the smallest, most innocent, and most unprotected among us. We can and must do better than this!

The Final Appeal

Ultimately, the fight for the right to live of each and every new life **in utero** is **the most significant human rights issue of our time!** Induced abortion is one of the most **vicious** and **violent** solutions to a complex set of social problems that has ever been proposed. It represents the penultimate intrusion of **"the big bully against the weakest and most vulnerable among us."**

The recognition that life at all stages in the womb is precious and is able to make extraordinary contributions to our ability to love and to be loved, to bring about peace and to be at peace, to extract love in ways that only a very young and precious life is able to extract, and to express love in ways that can be boundlessly meaningful needs to be adopted unconditionally. As we move to recognize the human right to live, we **must also move out of lethalism** and install positive and meaningful solutions to really significant human problems. We can call it *Humana vita magna et pretiosa est (Human Life is great and precious),* or *Magna Vita* for short!

God bless all of us as we move in this direction!

CHAPTER 12
REFERENCES AND FOOTNOTES

1. *Roe v. Wade*, 314F. Supp. 1217, United States Supreme Court, No. 70-18, January 22, 1973.

2. *Doe v. Bolton*, 319F. Supp. 1048, United States Supreme Court, NO. 70-40, January 22, 1973.

3. Flanagan, Geraldine Lux: The First Nine Months of Life. Simon & Schuster, New York, NY, 1962, pp. 25, 26.

4. World Medical Association Bulletin, 1:22, 1949.

5. World Medical Association Bulletin, 2:5–34, January, 1950.

6. Ibid.

7. Declaration of Oslo, World Medical Association, 1970.

8. Hilgers TW: Disturbing Trends in the Healthcare of Women, Children and Families. In: Hilgers TW: The Medical and Surgical Practice of **NaProTECHNOLOGY**. Pope Paul VI Institute Press, Chapter 1, Omaha, NE 2004.

9. Hilgers, TW: Blinders, Beaufort Books, New York, 2018.

10. Amicus Brief of Certain Physicians, Professors, and Fellows of the ACOG in Support of Appellees. In the Supreme Court of the United States, October Term, 1971, No. 70-18, *Roe v. Wade* and 70-40 *Doe v. Bolton*.

Epilogue

"You may be a Grown-up Sperm or a Grown-up Egg, but I am Not!"

It has amazed me over the years how far clinical scientists and/or basic scientists will go to defend their positive endorsement of abortion or abortion-related medicine. A good example of this was published in the March 2017 issue of *Fertility & Sterility* which is the major journal of the American Society of Reproductive Medicine. The letter was written by Dr. R. J. Paulson and it was entitled, "The Unscientific Nature of the Concept that 'Human Life Begins at Fertilization' and Why it Matters."[1] What Dr. Paulson concluded regarding the ability to communicate so easily these days is that "unfortunately, one unintended consequence of our near instantaneous communication is the rapid proliferation and dissemination of misinformation and outright disinformation." Indeed, topics such as false or "fake" news are a common topic in today's news media.

The lay public is often confronted with "apparent scientific contradictions" and thus develops "skepticism about the scientific method, concludes that science, like the news media is not a reliable source of information. When we scientists do not speak up to correct the unscientific conclusions attributed to science, we are complicit in the spread of such disinformation, leading to the undermining of science credibility in general."

Dr. Paulson goes on to say that, "One observation that has been attributed to scientific consensus — one that is highly relevant to our field (ed. Dr. Paulson is an IVF doctor) — is the concept of 'human life begins at fertilization.' This statement is commonly referred to by religious organizations and is often cited as the basis for so-called personhood amendments, but the insertion that it is scientifically sound is incorrect. And although it is often offered in the context of abortion, it has profound ramifications for the treatment of infertility, particularly *in vitro* fertilization (IVF). We fertility doctors take extreme care to protect and nurture the preimplantation embryos in our incubators and cryo-tanks. We realize that in almost all cases, the aggregates of cells present the best chance for our infertile couples to realize their dream of building their families. However, handling an embryo with the potential to produce a pregnancy is not the same as handling a human life. If harm to a preimplantation embryo were to be considered the same as harm to a human being, then the demise of a preimplantation embryo — a not infrequent event *in vivo*, as well as in the IVF laboratory — might well be treated as a human death, perhaps manslaughter charges brought against the embryologist.

"What is scientifically incorrect about saying that human life begins at fertilization? First, it is a categorical designation in conflict with the scientific observation that life is a continuum. The egg cell is alive, and has the potential to become a zygote (a single-celled embryo) if it is appropriately fertilized and activated by a live sperm. If fertilization is successful and the genetic complement of the sperm is added to that of the egg, the resulting zygote is also alive. The zygote has the same size as the egg; other than for its new genotype, the cell (comprised of the cytoplasm and the rest) is nearly identical to the egg cell. From a biological perspective, no new life has been created."

"Second, 'human life' implies individuality, which is also not consistent with scientific observations. In the clinical practice of IVF, we often speak of preimplantation and embryos as individual entities with distinct qualities like a specific genotype (mosaicism notwithstanding) and morphologic and developmental characteristics. But at the same time, we realize that each of the totipotent cells that comprise these embryos is, at least theoretically capable of producing a complete new individual. Indeed, multiple individuals can arise from the implantation of a single embryo, as in the case of identical twins. Therefore we know that the preimplantation embryo is not actually an individual. The preimplantation embryo is essentially an aggregate of stem cells, which has the potential to produce a pregnancy, including placental and fetal tissues, assuming that it successfully implants in a receptive endometrium. It is only after implantation that the early embryo can further differentiate into the organized cell groups that enable the developing conceptus to progress further in embryonic and eventually fetal development."

"'Life begins at fertilization' may certainly be considered a religious concept; because religious ideas are based on faith, no further proof is necessary. It is pointless to use science as an argument against faith-based dictums. For example, it is also not in the realm of science to investigate the nature of life after death or the validity of holy books. The beginning of human life likewise occupies the legal realm, where line drawing can be essential to the application of civil and criminal law. But laws are created by legislators, not scientists. Many attempts have been made to legally define life as beginning at fertilization. Although the impetus of this type of legislation is likely religious, a supporting argument is often made that this is a scientific fact as well, which is in contradiction to the arguments presented here."

"In these interesting times of nearly instantaneous communication and unlimited information, scientific conclusions are easily drowned out by other opinions. It matters to our patients and to us how information about our field is presented in the lay media. We should not quietly ignore the multiple web sites, lay publications and other sources of information and claim there is scientific proof that life begins at fertilization. If we do not object, our silence will be interpreted as scientific validation of this wholly religious, entirely unscientific conclusion. We should not be complicit in the dissemination of this type of disinformation and more specifically, we should not acquiesce to the claim that the concept of 'life begins at fertilization' has a scientific basis."

In the May 2, 2017 issue of Fertility & Sterility, I responded to Dr. Paulson[2] in the following fashion:

"In this article of Dr. Paulson's, the author suggests that the statement of 'human life begins at fertilization' is a form of 'misinformation and outright disinformation' comparing it to 'fake' news. Dr. Paulson suggests that such statements suggest 'apparent scientific contradictions' and that the reader or listener may develop a skepticism about the scientific method, and concludes that science like the news media, is 'not a reliable source of information.' It should be noted that scientific journals are often replete with editorial and political spin, but this article does not appear to recognize this."

"Of course, Dr. Paulson relies on the well-worn refrain that this 'is commonly offered by religious organizations' and adds that 'the assertion that it is scientifically sound is incorrect.' He offers a concern for the work that he's involved in, the treatment of infertility and *in vitro* fertilization. He then suggests that 'fertility doctors take extreme care to protect and nurture the preimplantation embryos.' It is only, however, because they represent 'the best chance for infertile couples to realize their dream of building families.' While this is an 'apparently good reason,' it doesn't deal with the reality of the phrase, 'human life begins at fertilization.' He seems to be mostly concerned about the doctor being exposed to 'manslaughter' charges. I don't recall that that's ever happened."

"In justification for his thoughts, he specifically says that, 'It is in conflict with the scientific observation that life is a continuum.' This is one of the same arguments that the Supreme Court in *Roe v. Wade* used, so it sounds very familiar. Certainly *in a generic sense*, life is a continuum, but nobody's ever been talking about life as a generality, but rather the beginning of the life of an individual who never previously existed. His reasoning is based upon 'the egg cell is alive' and has the potential to become a 'zygote if it is appropriately fertilized and activated by live sperm.' And if all this happens, 'then the resulting zygote is also alive.' He tries to gain some strength in his argument by suggesting that 'the zygote is the same size as the egg other than for its new genotype, the cell ... is nearly identical to the egg cell. From a biological perspective, no new life has been created,' he says.

"It is truly difficult to make this argument seriously. I know for myself that **I'm not a grownup oocyte, nor am I a grownup sperm!** In fact, the genotype means everything to the individual human person and his/her phenotype. The fact that the size of the zygote is about the same size of the egg cell is irrelevant and very superficial. It defies the reality of the newly formed, never again to be duplicated, individual human life."

"It seems to me that to prove his thesis, he could report on his study of an evaluation of *in vitro* fertilization pregnancies with special reference to all those babies that were gestated and eventually delivered when the time from fertilization up to implantation is purposely excluded (or destroyed). I know of no such study that's ever been done, nor can I expect that it will be done. It is a little bit like saying that the first 10 to 15 cell divisions of an ovarian cancer are not really ovarian cancer."

"Dr. Paulson does make a stab at the idea of 'individuality' of these human lives by suggesting that 'multiple individuals can arise from the implantation of a single embryo, as in the case of identical twins.' Identical twins occur in 1 out of 270 births or 0.3% of the time, so in 99.7% of concepti, individualization does occur at the time of conception or fertilization. The mere fact that on rare occasions these things can happen does not mean that the whole of that process should be redefined because of a minority occurrence. It is an old argument that has lost a significant amount of substance over the last 40 or 50 years. Dr. Paulson appears to try to get through this by referring to them as 'totipotent cells' or even 'stem cells.' But you need to show me that a stem cell has ever developed into a human being. Yes, human tissue such as liver, kidney, thyroid, etc., but none of those are human persons. The person is the whole of the individual, not just its parts."

"So then, he ends up by saying 'life begins at fertilization may certainly be considered a religious concept; because religious ideas are based on faith, no further proof is necessary.' In a one-page opinion article he refers to religion or faith eight times showing his own bias or antagonism. However, in my religion, faith enlightens reason and reason enlightens faith.[3] The two are not completely separate from each other, although they do have different foci. There are definitely groups within the population, however, who have a significant antithesis to religious faith. These individuals have little idea what it means to have faith and they have persisted in their attempts to force their idea of morality on the rest of us."

Many years ago, I remember a noted gynecologic surgeon who testified that when he looked under the microscope at a human embryo, he could not see a human soul. At that he kind of chuckled because he felt he had a 'gotcha moment!' But nobody said you could see the human soul no matter how hard you looked. **To call this only religious is frankly ludicrous!** It is a kind of semantic gymnastics (and blind spot) that frankly our science does not need along with being highly judgmental and prejudicial. Catholics for a very long time have been made fun of by other scientists because of what they think is the Catholic's inability to do good science because their faith gets in the way. Ridicule is not a response so much as it is a reaction. But, in fact, Catholic or Christian and Jewish scientists and clinicians have made some very significant contributions through research in the medical and other sciences. An example of some of these individuals is shown in Table EPI-1a and EPI-1b.

Incidentally, my practice is devoted to patients who have infertility and our success rates are legitimately good by just looking for the underlying causes and treating them effectively. More of this will be coming out over the next several years. But the IVF doctors have given up on looking for the causes of infertility and they rarely deal with that reality. I see so many patients who have previously been through either failed IVF programs or IVF programs in which they were treated like someone on a conveyor belt. The time will come when more and more women and couples begin to realize this and see that there is an alternative; and then they may very well look back on this article that suggests that 'human life begins at fertilization' is an unscientific proposal and the whole picture will begin to come back together again.

At the publication of this book, over two years have now passed since my challenge to Dr. Paulson and the whole of the IVF world to show us how they can establish pregnancy without beginning with a fertilized ovum. If you eliminate the step between fertilization and implantation there will be no pregnancies or no baby. All you need to do is "skip over" the conception step. This is a denial of biological realism and puts us back in the pre- middle ages again. *In vitro* fertilization (IVF) is actually one of the most telling scientific proofs that an individual life begins at fertilization (like the name of this procedure — IVF — clearly supports). Of course, they could always change the name to IVIP (*in vitro* Implantation Procedure). Changing names has been used before putting the science into more confusion. They can then redefine everything, get it into the medical dictionaries to achieve a level of "certitude." But keep in mind that "a definition is no substitute for knowledge" (anonymous).[4]

TABLE EPI-1a

CATHOLIC AND DEVOUT CHRISTIAN SCIENTISTS WHO CONTRIBUTED IN MAJOR WAYS TO VARIOUS SCIENTIFIC ACCOMPLISHMENTS AND UNDERSTANDINGS[1, 2]

NAME	MAJOR WORK
Louis Pasteur[3]	Bacteria as a cause of disease; invented pasteurization
Johannes Keplar[4]	One of the most original and influential astronomers & mathematicians
Alexander Fleming[3]	Discovered penicillin
Sir Isaac Newton[4] (physicist)	Laws of Gravity
Fr. Nicolaus Copernicus[3] (Augustinian Monk)	The earth revolves around the sun
Robert Boyle[4]	Cofounder Royal Society in Britain – Boyle's Law
Fr. Giambattista Riccioli[3]	Field of Acceleration
Michael Faraday	Electricity & Magnetism
Fr. Roger Boscovich[3]	Founder of Modern Atomic Theory
William Thomson Kelvin[4]	An honored physicist and a revered scientist

1. Coren, Michael: Why Catholics are Right. McClelland & Stewart, A division of Random Hourse of Canada, Ltd, 2011. pp. 76-79
2. Coren, Michael: Heresy: Ten Lies They Spread about Christianity. McClelland & Stewart, Toronto, Ontario, Canada, 2012, pp. 153-168.
3. Catholic
4. Christian

TABLE EPI-1b

CATHOLIC AND DEVOUT CHRISTIAN SCIENTISTS WHO CONTRIBUTED IN MAJOR WAYS TO VARIOUS SCIENTIFIC ACCOMPLISHMENTS AND UNDERSTANDINGS[1, 2]

NAME	MAJOR WORK
Gregor Mendel (Catholic Monk)[3]	The Father of Genetics
Max Planck[4]	Father of Quantum Theory
Fr. Nicholas Steno[3]	One of the Founders of Geology
Fr. J.B. Macelwane[3]	Introduction to Theoretical Seismology
Dr. Jerome Lejeune[3]	Discovered the chromosomal defect associated with Down's Syndrome
Sir William Albert Liley[4]	Performed the first intrauterine transfusion (by amniocentesis) for the treatment of fetal anemia
Dr. Ian Donald[4]	Developed prenatal diagnosis by ultrasound
Other Catholic Scientists Contributed with "staggering success"	• Pendulum clocks • Pantographs • Barometers • Reflecting telescopes • Microscopes • Magnetism • Optics • Electricity • Saturn's Rings • The Andromeda Nebula
St. Paul VI, St. John Paul II, Benedict XVI	All encouraged science & research done within a moral framework

1. Coren, Michael: Why Catholics are Right. McClelland & Stewart, A division of Random Hourse of Canada, Ltd, 2011. pp. 76-79
2. Coren, Michael: Heresy: Ten Lies They Spread about Christianity. McClelland & Stewart, Toronto, Ontario, Canada, 2012, pp. 153-168.
3. Catholic
4. Not Catholic

EPILOGUE
REFERENCES

1. Paulson RJ: The Unscientific Nature of the Concept that "Human Life Begins at Fertilization" and Why it Matters. Fertil Steril, Vol. 107, Issue 3 pp. 566–567, March 2017.

2. Hilgers TW: A Response to Dr. Paulson. Fertil Steril Dialog www.fertstertdialog.com, May 2, 2017.

3. John Paul II, Encyclical Letter *Fides et Ratio,* September 14, 1998.

4. It should be noted that since this interchange was published in <u>Fertility and Sterility</u> over 2 years ago, **no** response to the author's (Dr. Hilgers) input has been logged.

Glossary

-A-

American College of Obstetricians & Gynecologists (ACOG): The ACOG is described as the "premier" professional organization for physicians who practice or specialize in obstetrics and gynecology. They were first established in 1951 and are the publishers of the "Green Journal" in Obstetrics & Gynecology. The College often publishes committee opinions and practice recommendations which in a significant way dictates the way obstetrics and gynecology is to be practiced. This poses some difficulties because they're not infallible recommendations, but sometimes are viewed as such because of the medicolegal structure in the United States. It often dictates the way a particular problem should be handled and it is according to the group of physicians (the Committee) who addresses these issues. Often it is their favorite approach to the treatment of a particular problem when in fact other approaches are at least as good, if not better. However, they are the only such organization of its kind. In order to be a member, you must be certified in obstetrics and gynecology and this is done through the completion of an accredited four-year residency program; taking both written and oral

Board examinations administered by the American Board of Obstetrics & Gynecology (a separate organization).

abortion: The termination of a pregnancy either spontaneous or induced, accompanied by, resulting in, or closely followed by the death of the fetus.

Amicus Curiae: One (such as a professional person or organization) that is not a party to a particular litigation but that is permitted by the court to advise it in respect to some matter of law that directly affects the case in question; sometimes referred to in English as "Friend of the Court."

amniocentesis: Percutaneous transabdominal puncture of the uterus usually by needle to obtain amniotic fluid for testing.

ampicillin: A semisynthetic penicillin antibiotic effective orally against many gram-negative and gram-positive bacteria.

anatomy: The branch of science concerned with the bodily structures of humans, animals, and other living organisms.

arbitrary: Existing or coming about seemingly at random or by chance or as a capricious and unreasonable act of will.

Aristotle: (384–322 B.C.) Ancient Greek philosopher and scientist.

asters: A structure occurring in dividing cells, composed of microtubules radiating from a centrosome. The two asters are the poles of the spindle apparatus.

astronomer: An expert in or student of astronomy, the branch of science that deals with celestial objects, space.

atomic theory: The theory that all matter is made up of tiny indivisible particles (atoms).

-B-

bias: An inclination of temperament or outlook especially a personal and sometimes unreasoned judgment that influence decision making.

biology: The science that deals with the phenomena of life and living organisms in general.

Blackmun, Justice Harry: (1908–1999) Harry Andrew Blackmun was an American lawyer and jurist who served as an Associate Justice of the Supreme Court of the United States from 1970 until 1994. Best known as the author of the Court's opinion in *Roe v. Wade* and *Doe v. Bolton*.

blastocysts: A cluster of cells representing multiple cell divisions that have occurred in the fallopian tube after successful fertilization of an ovum by a sperm.

blastomere: A cell formed by cleavage of a fertilized ovum.

Blechschmidt, Erich: (1904–1992) was a German anatomist and director of Göttingen University's Anatomical Institute from 1942 until 1973. He held theories for embryogenesis based upon "morphogenetic fields" and also believed that more than just genes might act to control development.

Bolshevik: A member of the majority faction of the Russian Social Democratic Party, which was renamed the Communist Party after seizing power in the October Revolution of 1917.

Boyle's Law: An experimental gas law that describes how the pressure of a gas tends to increase as the volume of the container decreases.

Brown, Helen Gurley: (1922–2012) Helen Gurley Brown was an American author, publisher, and businesswoman. She was the editor-in-chief of Cosmopolitan magazine for 32 years.

-C-

cadaverous: Resembling a cadaver; dead body.

Calderone, MD, Mary S.: (1904–1998) A physician and a public health advocate for sex education. She helped overturn the American Medical Association policy against the dissemination of birth control information to patients.

California Medical Association: A professional organization representing physicians in California.

caudal: In a direction toward the buttocks.

cherry-pick: Choose and take only (the most beneficial, profitable or persuasive items, opportunities, etc.) from what is available.

chorioamnionitis: Inflammation of fetal membranes often associated with infection.

cleavage: The series of synchronized mitotic cell divisions of the fertilized egg that results in the formation of the blastomeres and changes the single-celled zygote into a multicellular embryo.

compendium: A brief summary of a larger work or of a field of knowledge.

conception: the beginning of human life when a new human being comes into existence marked by biologic union of the father's sperm and the mother's egg.

Condic, PhD, Maureen L.: A bioethicist, professor, ombudsman, and appointee to the United States National Science Board. Fields: bioethics, fetal development, spinal cord regeneration.

congeries: A disorderly collection; a jumble.

Constitution, United States: The United States Constitution (1789) is the supreme law of the United States. The Constitution, originally comprising seven articles, delineates the national frame of government.

Cosmopolitan Magazine (Cosmo): Cosmopolitan has since the 1960s been a women's magazine discussing such topics as sex, health, fitness, and fashion.

criminal abortion: An abortion that does not conform to statutory provisions governing the performance of abortions (sometimes referred to as "back-alley abortions").

-D-

deceptive: Giving an appearance or impression different from the true one; misleading.

Declaration of Geneva: The Declaration of Geneva was adopted by the General Assembly of the World Medical Association at Geneva in 1948, amended in 1968, 1983, 1994, editorially revised in 2005 and 2006 and amended in 2017.

It is a declaration of a physician's dedication to the Humanitarian goals of medicine. A declaration that was especially important in view of the medical crimes which had just been committed in German-occupied Europe. The Declaration of Geneva was originally intended as a revision of the Hippocratic Oath to a formulation of that oath's moral truths that could be comprehended and acknowledged in a modern way.

Declaration of Oslo: A statement by the World Medical Association in 1970—amended in 1983—which attempted to modernize the Hippocratic Oath's language on abortions regarding a woman's right to privacy.

dehumanization: To deprive of human qualities, personality, or spirit.

disputation: The action of disputing; verbal controversy.

DNA typing: A catch-all term for a wide range of methods for studying genetic variations.

Doe v. Bolton: The Doe v. Bolton case (January 22, 1973) defined the "health of the mother" in such a way that any abortion for any reason could be protected by the language of the decision. Its definition of health includes "all factors—physical, emotional, psychological, familial, and the woman's age—relevant to the well-being of the patient."

Down Syndrome: A chromosomal condition that is associated with intellectual disability, a characteristic facial appearance, and weak muscle tone (hypotonia) in infancy. All affected individuals experience cognitive delays, but the intellectual disability is usually mild to moderate.

dragooned: Coerce (someone) into doing something.

-E-

economic: Relating to economics or the economy; justified in terms of profitability.

Edelstein, Ludwig: (1902–1965) was a classical scholar and historian of medicine. Edelstein's 1943 translation and commentary on the Hippocratic Oath was about medical ethics.

egalitarian: Asserting, promoting, or marked by egalitarianism — a belief in human equality especially with respect to social, political, and economic affairs.

egg cell: Ovum; a female gamete.

embryo: The developing human individual from the time of implantation to the end of the eighth week after conception.

embryologic: Related to embryology.

embryology: A branch of biology dealing with embryos and their development.

equatorial plate: The central plane of the spindle in a dividing cell, to which chromosomes migrate during the metaphase of mitosis or meiosis.

expat: A person who lives in a foreign country.

-F-

fabricated: To make up for the purpose of deception.

factual: Of or relating to facts.

fake: Not true, real, or genuine.

fake science: Scientific deductions or conclusions not based on scientific facts or a misrepresentation of them.

farrago: An assortment or a medley; a conglomeration.

ferrets: A domesticated mustelid mammal with an elongated flexible body, often kept as a pet and sometimes trained to hunt rats or rabbits.

fertilization: The process by which the male's sperm unites with the female's oocyte, creating a new life.

fertilized egg: The cell resulting from union of a male and a female gamete: the fertilized ovum; zygote.

fetal age: The age of the conceptus computed from the time elapsed since fertilization.

fetology: The branch of medicine dealing with the fetus in utero.

fetus: The developing young in the uterus, specifically the unborn offspring in the postembryonic period, which in humans is from the third month after fertilization until birth.

Flanagan, Geraldine Lux: Author of "The First Nine Months of Life" 1962.

Frampton, Jr., George: Harvard law clerk (1971) for Justice Harry Blackmun helped research and draft opinion for Roe v. Wade.

Friedan, Betty: (1921–2006) An American feminist writer and activist. A leading figure in the women's movement. Author of The Feminine Mystique.

-G-

Galen: Galen of Pergamon, was a Greek physician, surgeon and philosopher in the Roman Empire.

generic: Characteristic of or relating to a class or group of things; not specific.

genetics: The study of genes and their heredity.

genotype: The entire genetic constitution of an individual

gentamycin: A bactericidal antibiotic that is used to treat severe or serious bacterial infections.

geology: A science that deals with the history of the earth and its life especially as recorded in rocks.

gestation: The period of development in the uterus until birth counted from the first day of a woman's last menstrual period.

gravity: The force that attracts a body toward the center of the earth.

Guttmacher, MD, Alan: (1898–1974) An American obstetrician-gynecologist who served as President of Planned Parenthood (1962–1968).

-H-

Hippocratic Oath: This is an oath historically taken by physicians. It is one of the most widely known of Greek medical texts. In its original form, it requires a new physician to swear to uphold specific ethical standards. The Oath is the earliest expression of medical ethics in the Western world.

Hooker, Davenport, PhD: University of Pittsburgh School of Medicine, a PhD gross anatomist. In January 1939 made film, "Early Fetal Human Activity" which showed fetuses response to outside stimuli in ages 8.5 to 14 weeks gestation.

human being: a man, woman, or child (including the unborn) of the species Homo sapiens.

Human-Embryological Documentation Collection: From the years "1930 to 1972, most especially at the Anatomical Institute of the University of Göttingen, West Germany," the embryologist, Professor E. Blechschmidt assembled the Blechschmidt Human-Embryological Documentation Collection in which he developed methods of human embryo reconstruction from serial sections and generated large models describing the embryonic period of human development.

Humanist Manifesto I: Also known as Humanist Manifesto I to distinguish it from later Manifestos in the series, was written in 1933 primarily by Raymond Bragg and published with 34 signers. Unlike the later manifestos, this first talks of a new religion and refers to humanism as a religious movement meant to transcend and replace previous, deity-based systems.

Hunter, Dr. William: (1718–1783) Anatomist and physician. Wrote a definitive work of his time, "The Anatomy of the Human Gravid Uterus" in 1774 which showed some of the most beautiful drawings of the growth and development of the baby in utero from the very earliest days of development through the time of birth. Was the physician to the Queen.

-I-

Illegal abortion: An abortion performed contrary to the laws regulating abortion.

implantation: Attachment of the blastocyst to the endometrium, and its subsequent embedding in the compact layer, occurring about 6–7 days after fertilization of the oocyte in humans.

in vitro fertilization: In vitro fertilization (IVF) is a procedure in which the eggs (ova) from a woman's ovary are removed. They are fertilized with sperm in a laboratory procedure, and then the fertilized egg (embryo) is returned to the woman's uterus.

International Code of Medical Ethics: The International Code of Medical Ethics was adopted by the third General Assembly of the World Medical Association (WMA) at London in 1949, and amended in 1968 and 1983.

investigation: A careful examination or search in order to discover facts or gain information.

-J-

Johns Hopkins University: The Johns Hopkins University is an American private research university in Baltimore, Maryland. Founded in 1876, the university was named for its first benefactor, the American entrepreneur, abolitionist, and philanthropist Johns Hopkins.

-L-

Lader, Lawrence: (1919–2006) He, along with Dr. Bernard Nathanson, were two of the founders of the pro-abortion group NARAL. Betty Friedan described him as "the founding father of the abortion movement."

Lethalism: the solution of complex social problems by killing the "human problem."

Lethalist: An individual who supports and/or participates in lethal solutions to complex social problems.

ludicrous: So foolish, unreasonable, or out of place as to be amusing; ridiculous.

-M-

malignant tumor: Cancerous growth.

Margaret Sanger Research Bureau: The Margaret Sanger Research Bureau (MSRB) began as the Clinical Research Bureau in 1923, which operated under the direction of the American Birth Control League (ABCL). In 1928, Sanger resigned as president of the ABCL and assumed full control of the clinic, renaming it the Birth Control Clinical Research Bureau (BCCRB).

maternal mortality rate: Defined as the number of maternal deaths during a given time period per 100,000 live births during the same time period.

mathematician: An expert in or student of mathematics.

Mayo Clinic: An integrated clinical practice, education and research institution specializing in diagnosing and treating patients, located in Rochester, Minnesota.

Means, Jr., Cyril: Law professor from New York University Law School — Professor Cyril Means, Jr., also became involved and was an attorney for NARAL.

medicine: The art and science of the diagnosis and treatment of disease and the maintenance of health.

meiosis: The process of cell division by which reproductive cells (gametes) are formed.

microscope: An instrument used to obtain an enlarged image of small objects and reveal details of structure not otherwise distinguishable.

morphological: Pertaining to the science of the forms and structure of organisms.

-N-

Nathanson, MD, Bernard: (1926–2011) An American medical doctor and co-founder in 1969 of the National Association for the Repeal of Abortion Laws — NARAL — later renamed National Abortion Rights Action League; became pro-life activist later in life and produced an ultrasound film called The Silent Scream.

neurobiology: The biology of the nervous system.

new embryological data: A term used by Justice Harry Blackmun to support his conclusion that "conception is a process over time rather than an event" while rejecting conception as the beginning of life.

Niswander, MD, Kenneth R.: A pro-abortion obstetrician-gynecologist practicing in Davis, CA.

noxious: hurtful; injurious; pernicious.

-O-

obstetrics: That branch of surgery which deals with the management of pregnancy, labor and delivery.

ontogenesis: Relating to the development of the individual organism; development of the individual, as distinguished from phylogeny, which is evolutionary development of the species.

ovaries: The female gonad: sexual glands in which the ova are formed.

ovum: The female reproductive or germ cell which after fertilization is a new member of the same species; called also an egg and sometimes loosely used in reference to the early stages of cellular division prior to implantation.

-P-

paradox: A statement that seems to contradict itself but may nonetheless be true.

pasteurization: The process of heating milk or other liquids, e.g., wine or beer, to destroy microorganisms that would cause spoilage.

peer-review: Appraisal by professional coworkers of equal status of the way an individual health professional conducts practice, education, or research.

penicillin: Originally, an antibiotic substance obtained from the cultures of certain molds; mainly bactericidal.

perinatology: The branch of medicine (obstetrics and pediatrics) dealing with the fetus and infant during the perinatal period (shortly before and after birth).

pernicious: Having a harmful effect, especially in a gradual or subtle way.

phenotype: The outward, visible expression of the hereditary constitution of an organism.

philosophy: The love or pursuit of knowledge and development of thinking.

physicians: An authorized practitioner of medicine, as one graduated from a college of medicine or osteopathy and licensed by the appropriate board.

Planned Parenthood: A non-profit organization that provides birth control in the United States and other countries. It is the largest provider of abortion in America.

Planned Parenthood Federation: Planned Parenthood Federation of America, Inc. (PPFA), formal name of Planned Parenthood. PPFA has its roots in Brooklyn, New York, where Margaret Sanger opened the first birth control clinic in the United States in 1916.

polar body: Either of two small cells produced during the first and second meiotic divisions in the development of an oocyte, containing little cytoplasm and eventually degenerating.

polarization: The presence or absence of polarity: the condition of having or exhibiting opposite effects at two extremities.

pornography: Writings, pictures, films, etc, designed to stimulate sexual excitement.

Posterity Clause: In the Preamble of the United States Constitution. The framers wanted this document to contain a most important reaffirmation of the present generation's responsibility to future generations.

pre-medieval era: It is the period in which Greek and Roman society flourished and wielded great influence throughout Europe, North Africa and the Middle East. Thought to be the period prior to the "middle ages."

prenatal: Existing or occurring before birth.

proletariat: Working class people.

psychological: Pertaining to psychology; the science that deals with the mind.

Pythagoreans: Originated in the 6th century BC, based on the teachings and beliefs held by Pythagorus and his followers. They espoused a rigorous life of the intellect and strict rules on diet, clothing and behavior.

-Q-

quadrille: A square dance in 6/8 or 2/4 time of French origin.

quantum theory: A theory for predicting the discrete energy states of atoms and of radiation.

quickening: The first recognizable movements by the mother of the fetus, usually appearing after the 18th week of gestation.

-R-

relativism: The idea that points of view are relative to differences in perception and consideration. No absolute or even near absolutes exist within this framework.

rheumy: Describing a watery discharge from the mucous membranes of eyes or nose.

Roe v. Wade: A landmark court decision in the United States issued by the Supreme Court of the United States in 1973 on the issue of the constitutionality of laws that criminalized or restricted access to abortions.

-S-

scientific fact: An observation that has been confirmed repeatedly and is accepted as true.

scientific reality: The quality or state of being actual or true.

segmentation: Division into similar parts.

seismology: The geophysical science of earthquakes and the mechanical properties of the earth.

semen: The penile ejaculate; a thick, yellowish-white, viscid fluid containing sperm.

settled science: Established science.

social abortion: The rejection of a pregnant woman by those close to her, such as boyfriend, husband, friends, relatives, physicians, etc. Most medical abortions are preceded by this rejection, placing pressure on her to abort the pregnancy due to a lack of support.

Soranus of Ephesus: (1st/2nd century A.D.) Soranus of Ephesus was a Greek physician. Several of his writings still survive, most notably his four-volume treatise on gynecology.

soul: The spiritual principle embodied in human beings.

sperm cell: The male gamete or sex cell that contains the genetic information to be transmitted by the male.

spermatozoan: The male reproductive cell; the male gamete.

spindle: A cytoplasmic network composed of microtubules along which the chromosomes are distributed during mitosis and meiosis.

squads: A small group of people organized in a common endeavor or activity.

St. Augustine: (354–430 A.D.) St. Augustine of Hippo, Doctor of the Church, bishop, philosopher, theologian.

St. Thomas Aquinas: (1225–1274) An Italian Dominican friar, Catholic priest and Doctor of the Church; an immensely influential philosopher, theologian and jurist.

-T-

testicles: Also called testes or gonads, they are part of the male reproductive system.

theologians: Persons versed in or engaged in the study of theology.

theology: The study of the nature of God and religious truth.

Tietze, MD, Christopher: (1908–1984) Biostatistician — Christopher Tietze was a United States physician best known for his stance in the United States movement to permit abortion and contraception in the United States.

tsunami: A great sea wave produced especially by submarine earth movement or volcanic eruption.

-U-

Unitarian Universalist Association: The UUA is a syncretistic religious group with liberal leanings; an association of congregations.

United Nations: Established in 1945, it is an intergovernmental organization with 193 member states. Its objectives include maintaining international peace and security, protecting human rights, delivering humanitarian aid, promoting sustainable development and upholding international law.

United Nations, General Assembly: The United Nations General Assembly is one of the six principal organs of the United Nations; the only one in

which all member nations have equal representation, and the main delib-
erative, policy-making, and representative organ of the UN.

uterus: A hollow muscular organ located in the pelvic cavity of female
mammals in which the fertilized egg implants and develops.

-V-

viability: Capability of living; the state of being viable; usually connotes
a fetus that has reached 500 g in weight and 20 gestational weeks'
development (18 weeks after fertilization). Can also be subdivided into
intracorporeal and *extracorporeal* viability

vintage: Characterized by excellence, maturity, and enduring appeal; classic.

vitellus: The stored nutrient of the ovum, the yolk.

-W-

Williams, Glanville: (1911–1997) a British authority on criminal law who
taught at Cambridge and also was a visiting professor at Columbia and
New York University. Was a pro-abortion leader in Great Britain in the
1950s and 1960s

World Medical Association: The World Medical Association (WMA) is an
international and independent confederation of free professional medical associations representing physicians worldwide; established 1947.

-X-

-Y-

-Z-

Zygote: The originating cell resulting from the union of a male and a female
gamete. Ultimately the initiating cell for all developmental phases and

stages of human development that are genetically unique in the growth and development of the human person.

Index

Shettles, LB, beginning of life, 49
single cell, v
Single Most Important Human
        Cell (SMIHC), 51 ff
social abortion, 26, 42, 43
"social arguments," 42
"social consequences," 42
Soranus of Ephesus, 8, 9
soul, 22, 37
sperm cell discovery, iv
sperm survival, 39
sperm, grown up, 137 ff
St. Augustine, iv, 8, 9
St. Thomas Aquinas, iv, 8, 9
Starling, Ernest, 12
Steno of Copenhagen, 12
Steves, Norman St. John, 36 ff
stylized drawing of unborn, 9
Subverted, 91
summary of investigation, 123 ff

T

Tietze, Christopher, 90
trimesters, 18

U

United Nations, vi
uterus, oldest known drawing
        of Soranus, iii

V

van Leeuwenhoek, Anton, iv, 12
viability, 111 ff
viability, extracorporeal, 112
viability, intracorporeal, 112
von Baer, Karl Ernst, 12

W

well-known facts of fetal development, v
What has been lost?, 126
Williams, Glanville, 36 ff, 40
Williams Obstetrics, 17, 18
World Medical Association, vi, vii, 10, 101

Z

zygote, 129

About the Author

Thomas W. Hilgers, MD

Director of the Saint Paul VI Institute for the Study of Human Reproduction in Omaha, Nebraska and the Medical Director of its nationally-accredited reproductive ultrasound center that features 3-D and 4-D ultrasound imaging. He began his first research in human fertility in 1968 as a senior medical student. Working at St. Louis University and Creighton University Schools of Medicine, he and his co-workers developed the **CREIGHTON MODEL Fertility*Care*™ System** and the new women's health science of **NaProTECH-NOLOGY®**. Those intrinsically involved in the development of the CrMS for the last 41 years, along with Dr. Hilgers are: K. Diane Daly, RN, CFCE; Susan K. Hilgers, BA, CFCE, and Ann M. Prebil, RN, BSN, CFCE (1946–2017).

Dr. Hilgers is currently a Senior Medical Consultant in Obstetrics, Gynecology, Reproductive Medicine and Surgery at the Saint Paul VI Institute and is a Clinical Professor in the Department of Obstetrics & Gynecology at Creighton University School of Medicine. He is Director of the Institute's Academic Programs and its National Center for Procreative Health. He is board certified in obstetrics, and gynecology, gynecologic laser surgery and is a member of the Society of Reproductive Surgeons and the Society of Procreative Surgeons. Furthermore, he is certified by the American Academy of FertilityCare Professionals (AAFCP) as a FertilityCare™ Medical Consultant (CFCMC) and Educator (CFCE).

He is the author of over 238 professional books, book chapters, poster sessions, articles, videotapes and he has given countless numbers of professional presentations. He has also been the recipient of 17 special recognition awards and 7 research awards. He also directs the largest annual CME program at Creighton University School of Medicine (132 hours per year). He is the recipient of 3 honorary doctorates and was named the Physician of the Year by the Nebraska Family Council.

Acknowledgements

The author wants to specifically acknowledge the role of Terri Green in the preparation of the manuscript with special emphasis on the development of the glossary. Matt Johnson was responsible for the layout and cover design. Thanks to both of them for their important contributions.

ANSWERS TO QUESTIONS:

1. Pig
2. Monkey
3. Feet from   A. Pig
                B. Monkey
                C. Human
4. Elephant

ALL IN A PHASE OF
INTRAUTERINE GROWTH
AND DEVELOPMENT, EASILY
RECOGNIZABLE BY A GROUP
OF 5 YEAR OLD CHILDREN!